I0625256

# Joy

Unlock the Secret to Lasting Happiness and Fulfillment:
Discover the Transformative Power of Joy in Every Aspect
of Your Life with this Comprehensive Self-Help Guide!

Lance P. Richards

Joy: Unlock the Secret to Lasting Happiness and Fulfillment: Discover the Transformative Power of Joy in Every Aspect of Your Life with this Comprehensive Self-Help Guide!

Copyright © 2023 - All rights reserved. No part of this book may be reproduced in any form or by any means without permission in writing from the publisher, LPR Publishing. Please read the full disclaimer at the end of this book.

# Table of Contents

# 01: Introduction: The Importance of Joy in Your Life

Joy is an essential aspect of human experience. It is a feeling of happiness and contentment that arises from within us when we experience positive emotions such as love, gratitude, and peace. Joy is different from happiness, which is often dependent on external circumstances, such as achievements, possessions, and status. Joy, on the other hand, is a state of being that arises from within us and is independent of external factors.

The importance of joy in our lives cannot be overstated. Joy brings us a sense of purpose, meaning, and fulfillment. It makes us feel alive and connected to the world around us. Joy enhances our physical and mental health, and it strengthens our relationships with others. Joy gives us the energy and motivation we need to pursue our goals and dreams.

Unfortunately, many of us have lost touch with joy in our lives. We live in a world that is often stressful, demanding, and chaotic. We are bombarded with negative news and images that can make it difficult to feel joy. We may have experienced trauma, loss, or other difficult life events that have dampened our ability to experience joy. We may have developed negative thought patterns or limiting beliefs that block our joy.

The good news is that joy is a natural human emotion that can be cultivated and nurtured. We can learn to reconnect with joy in our lives and experience its transformative power. In this comprehensive self-help guide, we will explore the many facets of joy and how it can be integrated into every aspect of your life.

We will begin by examining the concept of joy and what it means to experience joy. We will explore the science of joy and how it affects our brain and body. We will look at the benefits of joy, including its impact on our physical and mental health. We will also examine the barriers to joy, including negative emotions and thought patterns, and explore strategies for overcoming these barriers.

Next, we will explore how joy can be cultivated in different areas of our lives. We will examine how joy can be experienced in relationships, at work, in parenting, in communication, in self-care, in nature, in gratitude, in mindfulness, in creativity, in movement, in spirituality, in giving, and in re-

# 01: INTRODUCTION: THE IMPORTANCE OF JOY IN YOUR LIFE

silience. We will also explore how joy can be experienced in simple pleasures, such as eating, sleeping, traveling, and reflecting.

Throughout this guide, we will provide practical tips, exercises, and tools for cultivating joy in your life. We will also draw on real-life examples and stories from people who have experienced the transformative power of joy.

By the end of this guide, you will have a comprehensive understanding of joy and its impact on your life. You will have the tools and strategies you need to cultivate joy in every aspect of your life. You will be able to experience the transformative power of joy and unlock the secret to lasting happiness and fulfillment.

# 02: What is Joy? Understanding the Concept of Joy

Joy is a complex and multifaceted emotion that has been studied by philosophers, psychologists, and neuroscientists for centuries. Although joy is a universal human experience, it is difficult to define and understand because it is subjective and can be influenced by individual experiences and cultural contexts.

At its core, joy is a positive emotional experience that is characterized by feelings of happiness, pleasure, and contentment. It is often accompanied by a sense of connection, meaning, and purpose. Joy can be experienced in response to a wide range of stimuli, including relationships, achievements, nature, creativity, and spirituality.

One of the key features of joy is its transitory nature. Unlike happiness, which is often conceptualized as a stable and enduring state of well-being, joy is a more fleeting and ephemeral emotion. It can be experienced in moments of intense pleasure, such as winning a game or receiving a compliment, but it can also be felt in quieter moments of contentment, such as cuddling with a loved one or watching a beautiful sunset.

Another important feature of joy is its relationship to other positive emotions. Joy is often intertwined with feelings of gratitude, love, and awe. It can also be accompanied by other positive emotions, such as excitement, amusement, and pride. Joy can also enhance our experience of other positive emotions, making them feel more intense and meaningful.

The experience of joy can be influenced by a variety of factors, including our personality traits, cognitive processes, and social environments. For example, people who are more extraverted and open to new experiences may be more likely to experience joy in response to novel stimuli. Individuals who have a positive outlook on life and who are resilient in the face of adversity may also be more likely to experience joy in difficult situations.

Cognitive processes, such as attention and appraisal, also play a role in the experience of joy. People who are able to focus their attention on positive aspects of their lives and who are skilled at reappraising negative situations in a positive light may be more likely to experience joy. Similarly, people who have a sense of purpose and meaning in their lives may be more likely to experience joy because they are able to see their experiences as part of a larger, meaningful whole.

Social factors, such as social support and cultural norms, can also influence the experience of joy. People who have strong social networks and who feel connected to others may be more likely to experience joy in their relationships. Cultural norms and values can also shape our experience of joy by influencing what we find meaningful and pleasurable.

Despite the many factors that influence the experience of joy, it is a natural and essential human emotion that can be cultivated and nurtured. In the following chapters, we will explore strategies and techniques for cultivating joy in different aspects of our lives, including relationships, work, parenting, communication, self-care, nature, gratitude, mindfulness, creativity, movement, spirituality, giving, and resilience. By understanding the concept of joy and its many facets, we can learn to unlock the transformative power of joy and experience lasting happiness and fulfillment.

# 03: The Science of Joy: How Joy Affects Our Brain and Body

Joy is not just a subjective emotional experience, it is also a complex neurobiological phenomenon that has been the subject of much scientific study. Neuroscientists have found that joy involves complex interactions between different regions of the brain and various neurotransmitters and hormones that affect our mood, cognition, and behavior.

One of the key regions of the brain involved in the experience of joy is the amygdala. The amygdala is a small almond-shaped structure located deep within the brain that is responsible for processing emotions, including joy. When we experience something pleasurable, such as eating a delicious meal or spending time with loved ones, the amygdala releases neurotransmitters like dopamine, serotonin, and endorphins, which produce feelings of pleasure and reward.

Other regions of the brain that are involved in the experience of joy include the prefrontal cortex, which is responsible for regulating emotions and decision-making, and the hippocampus, which is involved in memory and learning. Studies have shown that when we experience joy, these regions of the brain are activated, leading to improved cognit-

ive function, memory retention, and decision-making abilities.

In addition to its effects on the brain, joy also has a profound impact on our physical health and well-being. Research has shown that people who experience more joy and
positive emotions have lower levels of stress hormones like
cortisol, which can contribute to a variety of health problems, including cardiovascular disease, diabetes, and depression.

Joy also has a positive impact on our immune system, increasing the activity of natural killer cells and other immune
cells that help fight off infections and diseases. This is because the neurotransmitters and hormones released during
joyful experiences activate the parasympathetic nervous
system, which helps to counteract the negative effects of
stress on the body.

The effects of joy on the body are not limited to the immune
system. Joyful experiences have also been shown to improve sleep quality, lower blood pressure, and reduce inflammation, which is a key factor in many chronic diseases.

## 03: THE SCIENCE OF JOY: HOW JOY AFFECTS OUR BRAIN AND BODY

In addition to its physical effects, joy also has a powerful social impact. When we experience joy, we are more likely to connect with others and engage in prosocial behaviors, such as helping, sharing, and cooperating. This is because joy activates the reward centers of the brain, which reinforce these positive behaviors and promote social bonding.

The science of joy has important implications for our lives and well-being. By understanding the neurobiological underpinnings of joy, we can learn to cultivate and enhance this emotion in our daily lives. This can be achieved through a variety of practices, such as mindfulness, gratitude, positive thinking, social connections, and physical exercise.

By embracing joy and making it a priority in our lives, we can experience not only immediate feelings of happiness and contentment, but also long-term benefits for our physical and mental health. Joy has the power to transform our lives and the lives of those around us, making it a truly transformative emotion.

# 04: The Benefits of Joy: How Joy Improves Our Physical and Mental Health

Joy is not just a fleeting emotion that brings us temporary happiness; it also has numerous benefits for our physical and mental health. In fact, research has shown that experiencing joy on a regular basis can have a profound impact on our overall well-being and quality of life. In this chapter, we will explore some of the many ways in which joy can improve our physical and mental health.

One of the most well-known benefits of joy is its positive impact on our mood and emotional well-being. When we experience joy, we feel happy, content, and fulfilled, which can help to alleviate feelings of sadness, anxiety, and depression. Joy can also increase our resilience and coping skills, making it easier to deal with the challenges and stresses of daily life.

But the benefits of joy extend far beyond our emotional state. Joy has also been shown to improve our physical health in a number of ways. For example, studies have found that people who experience more joy and positive emotions have lower levels of inflammation, which is a key factor in many chronic diseases such as arthritis, diabetes, and heart disease.

Joy also has a positive impact on our cardiovascular system. When we experience joy, our bodies release hormones such as oxytocin, which can help to lower our blood pressure and reduce the risk of heart disease. In fact, studies have found that people who experience more joy and positive emotions have a lower risk of developing cardiovascular disease.

Joy can also improve our immune function, making us less susceptible to illness and disease. Research has shown that people who experience more joy and positive emotions have higher levels of natural killer cells, which play an important role in fighting off infections and cancer.

In addition to its physical benefits, joy can also improve our cognitive function and brain health. Studies have found that people who experience more joy and positive emotions have better memory, attention, and problem-solving skills. Joy has also been shown to increase the volume of gray matter in the brain, which is associated with improved cognitive function and reduced risk of dementia.

Finally, joy can have a positive impact on our social relationships and overall sense of well-being. When we experience joy, we are more likely to engage in social behaviors such as helping, sharing, and cooperating, which can strengthen our relationships and increase our sense of connection to others. Joy can also increase our sense of purpose and meaning in life, leading to greater feelings of fulfillment and satisfaction.

In summary, the benefits of joy are numerous and far-reaching. From improving our physical health to enhancing our emotional well-being and cognitive function, joy has the power to transform every aspect of our lives. By prioritizing joy and incorporating practices that cultivate this emotion into our daily routines, we can experience greater happiness, health, and fulfillment in our lives.

# 05: Barriers to Joy: Overcoming Negative Emotions and Mindsets

While joy can have numerous benefits for our physical and mental health, it can be difficult to experience this emotion on a regular basis. There are many barriers that can prevent us from feeling joyful, including negative emotions and mindsets that can be difficult to overcome. In this chapter, we will explore some of the common barriers to joy and provide strategies for overcoming them.

One of the biggest barriers to joy is negative emotions such as sadness, anger, and fear. These emotions can be overwhelming and make it difficult to experience joy in the present moment. One strategy for overcoming negative emotions is to practice mindfulness. Mindfulness involves being present in the moment, observing our thoughts and emotions without judgment, and accepting them as they are. By practicing mindfulness, we can learn to be more aware of our emotions and respond to them in a healthy and positive way, rather than getting stuck in negative thought patterns.

Another barrier to joy is negative self-talk and limiting beliefs. These beliefs can be deeply ingrained and difficult to overcome, but they can have a profound impact on our ability to experience joy. One strategy for overcoming limiting beliefs is to challenge them with evidence. For example, if you believe that you are not capable of achieving your goals, you can look for examples of times when you have succeeded in the past. By focusing on evidence that supports a more positive belief, we can begin to shift our mindset and open ourselves up to more joyful experiences.

Perfectionism is another barrier to joy that can prevent us from fully embracing our experiences. When we have rigid expectations of ourselves and our experiences, we can become disappointed and frustrated when things do not go as planned. One strategy for overcoming perfectionism is to practice self-compassion. Self-compassion involves treating ourselves with kindness and understanding, rather than harshly criticizing ourselves for our perceived flaws and shortcomings. By practicing self-compassion, we can learn to be more accepting of ourselves and our experiences, and open ourselves up to more joyful experiences.

Finally, another common barrier to joy is a lack of connection and community. When we feel isolated and disconnected from others, it can be difficult to experience joy in our lives. One strategy for overcoming this barrier is to focus on building strong and meaningful relationships with others. This can involve reaching out to friends and family, participating in community activities, or joining groups and organizations that align with our interests and values. By cultivating meaningful connections with others, we can increase our sense of belonging and enhance our ability to experience joy in our lives.

In summary, there are many barriers to joy that can prevent us from fully experiencing this emotion in our lives. By practicing mindfulness, challenging limiting beliefs, practicing self-compassion, and building meaningful connections with others, we can overcome these barriers and open ourselves up to more joyful experiences. With persistence and commitment, we can cultivate a more joyful and fulfilling life, filled with happiness, purpose, and meaning.

# 06: Cultivating Joy: Strategies for Nurturing Joy in Your Life

While joy can be elusive at times, it is possible to cultivate this emotion in our lives. In this chapter, we will explore some strategies for nurturing joy and experiencing more happiness and fulfillment in our daily lives.

– Practice Gratitude

Gratitude is one of the most powerful ways to cultivate joy in our lives. By focusing on what we are grateful for, we shift our attention away from negative thoughts and emotions, and cultivate a more positive outlook on life. Some ways to practice gratitude include keeping a gratitude journal, expressing gratitude to others, and focusing on the present moment.

– Engage in Activities That Bring You Joy

Engaging in activities that bring us joy is another powerful way to cultivate this emotion in our lives. Whether it's spending time in nature, pursuing a hobby, or spending time with loved ones, engaging in activities that bring us joy can help us feel more fulfilled and content.

## 06: CULTIVATING JOY: STRATEGIES FOR NURTURING JOY IN YOUR LIFE

– Practice Mindfulness

Mindfulness is another powerful tool for cultivating joy in our lives. By being fully present in the moment, we can cultivate a deeper appreciation for the simple pleasures in life, and experience more joy in our daily experiences. Mindfulness practices such as meditation, deep breathing, and body scans can help us cultivate greater awareness and presence in our lives.

– Practice Self-Care

Taking care of ourselves is another important aspect of nurturing joy in our lives. Self-care practices such as exercise, healthy eating, and adequate sleep can help us feel more energized and positive. Additionally, engaging in practices such as massage, acupuncture, or yoga can help us release tension and feel more relaxed and at ease.

– Build Meaningful Relationships

Strong and meaningful relationships are another important aspect of cultivating joy in our lives. Spending time with loved ones, volunteering in our community, and engaging in activities with others who share our interests and values can help us feel more connected and fulfilled.

– Practice Compassion

Finally, practicing compassion towards ourselves and others is another powerful tool for nurturing joy in our lives. When we treat ourselves and others with kindness and understanding, we create a positive and supportive environment that fosters joy and fulfillment. Practices such as loving-kindness meditation can help us cultivate greater compassion and empathy towards ourselves and others.

In summary, cultivating joy in our lives requires a commitment to practices such as gratitude, engaging in activities that bring us joy, practicing mindfulness and self-care, building meaningful relationships, and practicing compassion. By incorporating these practices into our daily lives, we can experience greater happiness, fulfillment, and joy in all aspects of our lives.

# 07: Joy in Relationships: How to Build and Sustain Joyful Relationships

Introduction

Joyful relationships are one of the most essential aspects of a fulfilling life. Relationships bring us love, connection, and companionship, and can significantly impact our well-being. However, building and sustaining joyful relationships can be a challenging task, requiring patience, understanding, and effort. In this chapter, we will explore the transformative power of joy in relationships, how to cultivate it, and the tools you need to sustain it.

The Importance of Joy in Relationships

Relationships can bring us great joy, but they can also be a source of stress, anxiety, and frustration. Building joyful relationships requires us to focus on the positive aspects of our connections with others, rather than dwelling on negative experiences. Studies show that joyful relationships can help us manage stress and increase overall well-being. In contrast, negative relationships can lead to depression, anxiety, and other mental health problems.

## 07: JOY IN RELATIONSHIPS: HOW TO BUILD AND SUS-
## TAIN JOYFUL RELATIONSHIPS

### The Role of Communication in Joyful Relationships

Communication is an essential tool for building joyful relationships. It is through communication that we express our
needs, wants, and feelings to others. However, communication can be tricky, and misunderstandings can lead to hurt
feelings, misunderstandings, and even relationship breakdowns. Effective communication requires active listening,
open-mindedness, and empathy.

### Active Listening

Active listening involves giving your full attention to the
person you are communicating with. It means paying attention to their words, body language, and tone of voice. By
actively listening, you can better understand the person's
needs, feelings, and thoughts. This, in turn, can help you respond in a way that is supportive and helpful, leading to
more positive and joyful interactions.

### Open-mindedness

Open-mindedness means being open to different ideas and
perspectives, even if they are different from our own. In re-

lationships, this means being willing to consider our partner's needs and desires, even if they do not align with our
own. Being open-minded can help us build stronger connections with others, fostering trust, and understanding.

Empathy

Empathy is the ability to understand and share the feelings
of others. By empathizing with our partners, we can better
understand their emotions, leading to more supportive and
compassionate interactions. Empathy helps us to connect
with others on a deeper level, creating more meaningful and
joyful relationships.

The Power of Gratitude in Relationships

Gratitude is an essential ingredient in building joyful relationships. Gratitude involves recognizing and appreciating
the positive aspects of our relationships, rather than focusing on the negative. Expressing gratitude can help us feel
more connected to our partners, leading to increased feelings of happiness and fulfillment.

Expressing gratitude can take many forms, such as saying

thank you, giving compliments, and expressing appreciation for the things our partners do. By expressing gratitude regularly, we can build stronger and more positive relationships, leading to greater levels of joy and fulfillment.

Overcoming Challenges in Relationships

No relationship is perfect, and every relationship will face challenges at some point. It is how we handle these challenges that will determine the strength and longevity of our relationships. Some common challenges that can arise in relationships include:

Communication Breakdowns

Communication breakdowns can occur when misunderstandings or conflicts arise. To overcome communication breakdowns, it is important to practice active listening, open-mindedness, and empathy. By doing so, we can better understand our partner's needs and desires, leading to more productive and positive interactions.

Conflict Resolution

Conflict is a natural part of any relationship. However, how we handle conflict can have a significant impact on the health of our relationships. To effectively resolve conflicts, it is important to remain calm, listen actively, and work collaboratively to find a solution that works for both parties. By doing so, we can build stronger and more resilient relationships.

Lack of Trust

If trust is broken in a relationship, it can be challenging to rebuild. However, it is possible to regain trust through open communication, honesty, and consistent actions that demonstrate a commitment to rebuilding trust. This can take time and effort, but it is worth it to build a stronger and more joyful relationship.

Tips for Building and Sustaining Joyful Relationships

– Practice Gratitude: Expressing gratitude regularly can help build stronger and more positive relationships, leading to increased feelings of happiness and fulfillment.

– Communicate Effectively: Effective communication is essential for building joyful relationships. Practice active

listening, open-mindedness, and empathy to better understand your partner's needs and desires.

– Spend Quality Time Together: Spending quality time together can help strengthen your relationship and foster feelings of closeness and connection.

– Show Affection: Small gestures of affection, such as hugs
and kisses, can help build intimacy and connection in relationships.

– Support Each Other: Supporting each other through both
good times and bad can help build trust, resilience, and a
stronger connection.

– Be Open and Honest: Being open and honest with your
partner can help build trust and foster more meaningful interactions.

– Practice Forgiveness: Forgiving your partner when they
make mistakes can help build a stronger and more resilient
relationship.

Conclusion

## 07: JOY IN RELATIONSHIPS: HOW TO BUILD AND SUSTAIN JOYFUL RELATIONSHIPS

Joyful relationships are a cornerstone of a fulfilling life. Building and sustaining joyful relationships requires effort, patience, and understanding. Effective communication, gratitude, affection, and support are all essential ingredients for building joyful relationships. By focusing on the positive aspects of our relationships and working together to overcome challenges, we can create stronger, more joyful, and fulfilling relationships.

# 08: Joy at Work: Creating a Joyful Workplace Environment

Introduction

Work can often feel like a chore, something that needs to be done to pay the bills. But it doesn't have to be that way. In fact, creating a joyful workplace environment can not only increase productivity and employee satisfaction but also lead to a more fulfilling and happy life. In this chapter, we'll explore the benefits of a joyful workplace environment and provide tips on how to create one.

Benefits of a Joyful Workplace Environment

– Increased Productivity: When employees are happy and engaged, they are more likely to be productive and produce high-quality work.

– Lower Turnover Rates: A joyful workplace environment can lead to increased job satisfaction and lower turnover rates.

– Improved Mental Health: A positive workplace culture can help reduce stress and anxiety, leading to improved mental health for employees.

## o8: JOY AT WORK: CREATING A JOYFUL WORKPLACE ENVIRONMENT

– Better Communication: A joyful workplace environment can foster better communication and collaboration among employees, leading to more efficient and effective teamwork.

– Increased Creativity: A joyful workplace environment can encourage creativity and innovation, leading to new and exciting ideas that can benefit the company.

Tips for Creating a Joyful Workplace Environment

– Encourage Positivity: Encourage employees to focus on the positive aspects of their work and celebrate successes, both big and small.

– Foster a Sense of Community: Encourage employees to connect with each other and build relationships through team-building activities, social events, and open communication.

– Provide Opportunities for Growth: Providing opportunities for professional development and growth can help employees feel valued and motivated.

– Recognize and Reward Achievements: Recognizing and

rewarding employees for their achievements can boost morale and increase job satisfaction.

– Create a Comfortable Physical Environment: Creating a comfortable physical environment, such as providing comfortable seating, adequate lighting, and a clean workspace, can help employees feel more relaxed and productive.

– Encourage Flexibility: Providing flexible work arrangements, such as telecommuting or flexible schedules, can help employees feel more in control of their work and personal lives.

– Support Employee Wellness: Encouraging employee wellness, such as providing healthy snacks, access to exercise facilities, and mental health resources, can help employees feel valued and supported.

Conclusion

A joyful workplace environment can benefit both employees and employers, leading to increased productivity, job satisfaction, and overall happiness. By fostering positivity, community, growth, recognition, comfort, flexibility, and wellness, you can create a workplace culture that is both joyful and productive. Remember, creating a joyful workplace environment is an ongoing process that requires effort, patience, and commitment. But the rewards are worth it.

# 09: Joyful Parenting: How to Foster Joy in Your Children's Lives

Introduction

Being a parent is one of the most fulfilling and rewarding experiences in life, but it can also be challenging at times. As parents, we want our children to be happy, healthy, and fulfilled. One way to achieve this is by fostering joy in their lives. In this chapter, we'll explore the benefits of joyful parenting and provide tips on how to foster joy in your children's lives.

Benefits of Joyful Parenting

– Increased Happiness: Fostering joy in your children's lives can lead to increased happiness and positive emotions.

– Improved Mental Health: Joyful parenting can help reduce stress and anxiety in children, leading to improved mental health.

– Better Relationships: When parents and children experience joy together, it can strengthen their bond and foster a deeper connection.

— Improved Behavior: Children who experience joy in their lives are more likely to exhibit positive behaviors, such as kindness and empathy.

— Increased Resilience: Fostering joy in your children's lives can help them develop resilience and the ability to cope with challenges.

Tips for Fostering Joy in Your Children's Lives

— Model Joyful Behavior: Children learn by example, so model joyful behavior by expressing gratitude, finding joy in everyday moments, and sharing your positive emotions with your children.

— Encourage Play and Creativity: Encourage your children to engage in play and creative activities, such as drawing, dancing, or playing games, as these can help foster joy and positive emotions.

— Connect with Nature: Spending time in nature can be a great way to foster joy in children's lives. Take your children on nature walks, go camping, or spend time exploring local parks and outdoor spaces.

– Create Positive Memories: Make an effort to create positive memories with your children by taking family trips, doing fun activities together, or celebrating special occasions.

– Practice Mindfulness: Encourage your children to practice mindfulness by focusing on the present moment and their surroundings, which can help foster joy and positive emotions.

– Foster Positive Relationships: Encourage positive relationships with family, friends, and community members, as these can provide a sense of connection and belonging.

– Show Unconditional Love and Support: Show your children unconditional love and support, even during difficult times. This can help them develop a sense of security and confidence, which can lead to increased joy and fulfillment.

Conclusion

Fostering joy in your children's lives can lead to increased happiness, improved mental health, better relationships, improved behavior, and increased resilience. By modeling joyful behavior, encouraging play and creativity, connecting with nature, creating positive memories, practicing mindfulness, fostering positive relationships, and showing unconditional love and support, you can create a joyful environment for your children to thrive in. Remember, joyful parenting is an ongoing process that requires effort, patience, and commitment, but the rewards are worth it.

# 10: Joyful Communication: Enhancing Your Communication Skills to Promote Joy

Introduction

Communication is an essential part of our daily lives. It is the foundation of our relationships with others and can greatly impact our levels of joy and fulfillment. Effective communication can help us build stronger connections with those around us, while poor communication can lead to misunderstandings, conflict, and stress. In this chapter, we will explore the role of communication in promoting joy and provide tips for enhancing your communication skills to promote more joyful interactions with others.

The Importance of Joyful Communication

Joyful communication is a critical component of building and maintaining positive relationships with others. It can help us express our emotions effectively, understand others' perspectives, and build trust and rapport. Additionally, joyful communication can lead to greater feelings of happiness and fulfillment in both ourselves and those around us.

# 10: JOYFUL COMMUNICATION: ENHANCING YOUR COMMUNICATION SKILLS TO PROMOTE JOY

Tips for Enhancing Your Communication Skills to Promote Joy

– Practice Active Listening: Active listening is a crucial part of effective communication. It involves fully focusing on the speaker, demonstrating empathy and understanding, and avoiding interruptions or distractions. When we actively listen to others, we show them that we value their thoughts and feelings, which can help build stronger connections and foster joy.

– Use Positive Language: The words we use can greatly impact the tone and mood of our conversations. Using positive language, such as "I appreciate," "I understand," and "I respect," can help create a more positive and joyful atmosphere. Conversely, negative language, such as "I can't," "I won't," and "I don't like," can lead to feelings of defensiveness and conflict.

– Practice Empathy: Empathy involves putting yourself in the other person's shoes and understanding their perspective. It can help you connect with others on a deeper level and foster greater feelings of joy and understanding. To practice empathy, try to see things from the other person's point of view and validate their feelings and experiences.

– Be Mindful of Nonverbal Cues: Nonverbal cues, such as facial expressions, body language, and tone of voice, can convey more than our words alone. Being mindful of your nonverbal cues can help ensure that your communication is positive and joyful. For example, smiling, maintaining eye contact, and using a friendly tone can help create a more positive and joyful atmosphere.

– Avoid Assumptions and Judgments: Making assumptions or judgments about others can lead to misunderstandings and conflict. Instead, try to approach conversations with an open mind and ask clarifying questions to better understand the other person's perspective.

– Express Gratitude: Expressing gratitude can help promote joy and positive emotions in both yourself and others. When you express gratitude, you acknowledge the value and importance of others in your life, which can help foster deeper connections and greater feelings of joy and fulfillment.

– Practice Patience and Understanding: Effective communication requires patience and understanding. It is important to take the time to listen to others, understand their perspective, and communicate in a way that is respectful and empathetic. This can help build trust and rapport and foster greater feelings of joy and positivity.

Conclusion

Joyful communication is a critical component of building and maintaining positive relationships with others. By practicing active listening, using positive language, practicing empathy, being mindful of nonverbal cues, avoiding assumptions and judgments, expressing gratitude, and practicing patience and understanding, you can enhance your communication skills to promote more joyful interactions with others. Remember, effective communication is an ongoing process that requires effort and commitment, but the rewards are worth it in the form of deeper connections, greater happiness, and more fulfilling relationships.

# 11: Joyful Self-Care: How to Prioritize Self-Care for Greater Joy and Fulfillment

In today's fast-paced and hectic world, it's easy to neglect our own needs and well-being in the pursuit of success and productivity. However, self-care is crucial for maintaining joy and fulfillment in every aspect of our lives. In this chapter, we will explore the importance of self-care and strategies for prioritizing self-care in your daily routine.

What is Self-Care?

Self-care refers to the intentional and proactive steps we take to maintain and improve our physical, mental, and emotional health. It's about prioritizing our own needs and well-being and ensuring that we are taking care of ourselves on a regular basis. Self-care looks different for everyone and can include activities such as exercise, healthy eating, meditation, and hobbies.

The Importance of Self-Care

Self-care is essential for maintaining joy and fulfillment in our lives. When we neglect our own needs, we become more vulnerable to stress, anxiety, and burnout. By prioritizing self-care, we can improve our physical health, boost our mood, and enhance our overall sense of well-being. Self-care also helps us to better manage our relationships and responsibilities, allowing us to show up as our best selves in every aspect of our lives.

Strategies for Prioritizing Self-Care

Incorporating self-care into our daily routines can be challenging, especially when we have busy schedules and competing demands. However, there are several strategies that can help us to prioritize self-care and make it a regular part of our lives:

– Schedule self-care: Set aside dedicated time for self-care activities in your daily or weekly schedule. Treat it as you would any other appointment or commitment.

– Identify your self-care needs: Take some time to reflect on what activities and practices bring you joy and help you to feel balanced and rejuvenated. Incorporate these activities into your self-care routine.

# 11: JOYFUL SELF-CARE: HOW TO PRIORITIZE SELF-CARE FOR GREATER JOY AND FULFILLMENT

– Practice self-compassion: Be kind and compassionate with yourself when you're feeling stressed or overwhelmed. Don't judge yourself for needing time to rest and recharge.

– Make self-care a priority: Remember that self-care is not selfish. Prioritizing your own well-being ultimately benefits those around you as well.

– Start small: Don't feel like you need to overhaul your entire routine all at once. Start with small, manageable steps and build from there.

Self-Care Activities to Try

There are countless self-care activities to explore, and what works best for you will depend on your preferences and needs. Here are a few ideas to get started:

– Mindfulness practices: Meditation, yoga, and deep breathing exercises can help to reduce stress and improve mental clarity.

– Exercise: Physical activity is not only good for our bodies, but also has been shown to improve mood and reduce stress.

## 11: JOYFUL SELF-CARE: HOW TO PRIORITIZE SELF-CARE FOR GREATER JOY AND FULFILLMENT

– Creative pursuits: Engaging in creative activities such as painting, writing, or playing music can be a great way to unwind and tap into your creativity.

– Socializing: Spending time with friends and loved ones can help to boost our mood and provide a sense of connection and support.

– Alone time: Taking some time to be alone and enjoy solitude can be an important way to recharge and reflect.

In conclusion, prioritizing self-care is essential for maintaining joy and fulfillment in every aspect of our lives. By taking intentional steps to care for ourselves, we can improve our overall sense of well-being and better manage the demands of daily life. Remember to be kind to yourself, identify your unique self-care needs, and make self-care a regular part of your routine.

# 12: Joy in Nature: Finding Joy and Connection in the Natural World

Introduction

In our modern world, it's easy to get caught up in our daily routines and forget about the natural world around us. However, studies have shown that spending time in nature can have numerous benefits, including reducing stress, improving mood, and increasing overall well-being. In this chapter, we'll explore the concept of joy in nature and how you can find greater joy and connection through spending time outdoors.

The Healing Power of Nature

Humans have an innate connection to nature that dates back to our earliest ancestors. Our bodies and minds are designed to function best when we are in natural environments. Studies have shown that exposure to natural settings can have a variety of positive effects on our health, including reducing stress levels, lowering blood pressure, and improving overall well-being.

Spending Time Outdoors

# 12: JOY IN NATURE: FINDING JOY AND CONNECTION IN THE NATURAL WORLD

There are many ways to spend time in nature, whether it's hiking through a national park, taking a walk in the woods, or simply sitting outside and enjoying the sunshine. The key is to find activities that you enjoy and that allow you to connect with the natural world around you. Even small doses of nature can have a positive impact on your mental health, so it's important to make time for outdoor activities whenever possible.

Connecting with Nature

One of the most important aspects of finding joy in nature is learning to connect with the natural world around you. This can be done in a variety of ways, from simply taking the time to notice the beauty of a sunrise or sunset, to learning about the plants and animals that live in your local environment. By connecting with nature on a deeper level, you can find greater joy and appreciation for the world around you.

The Benefits of Nature-Based Activities

There are many benefits to incorporating nature-based activities into your life. For example, research has shown that spending time in nature can improve your mood, boost your immune system, and even increase your creativity. Additionally, participating in outdoor activities can be a great way to get exercise, which is important for overall health and well-being.

## Making Nature a Priority

In order to experience the benefits of nature, it's important to make it a priority in your life. This may mean setting aside time each day to spend outdoors, or planning regular camping or hiking trips with friends and family. Whatever approach you take, it's important to remember that spending time in nature is an investment in your health and well-being.

## Conclusion

Finding joy in nature is an important part of living a fulfilling life. By spending time outdoors and connecting with the natural world around you, you can improve your physical and mental health, boost your mood, and find greater joy and fulfillment in your daily life. Whether it's taking a walk in the park or planning a camping trip, make sure to make nature a priority in your life and enjoy the many benefits that it has to offer.

# 13: The Power of Gratitude: How Gratitude Enhances Joy

## Introduction

Gratitude is a powerful emotion that can transform your life. It allows you to appreciate the good things in your life and find joy in everyday moments. When you cultivate gratitude, you open yourself up to experiencing more joy and fulfillment. In this chapter, we will explore the power of gratitude and how it enhances joy.

## The Definition of Gratitude

Gratitude is a feeling of appreciation or thankfulness for something that you have received or experienced. It is an acknowledgement of the good things in your life, both big and small. Gratitude is often described as an attitude or a state of mind that can be cultivated through intentional practices.

## The Benefits of Gratitude

Gratitude has been shown to have numerous benefits for mental and physical health. Studies have found that practicing gratitude can:

– Increase happiness and well-being: Grateful people tend to be happier and more content with their lives.

– Reduce stress and anxiety: Gratitude can help reduce feelings of stress and anxiety, as well as improve sleep quality.

– Boost resilience: Gratitude has been linked to greater resilience in the face of challenges and adversity.

– Improve relationships: Expressing gratitude towards others can strengthen relationships and increase feelings of connection and intimacy.

– Enhance empathy and compassion: Grateful people tend to be more empathetic and compassionate towards others.

Cultivating Gratitude

Gratitude can be cultivated through a variety of practices, such as:

– Gratitude journaling: Writing down things you are grateful for on a regular basis, such as every day or once a week.

– Gratitude letters: Writing a letter to someone expressing

gratitude for something they have done for you.

– Gratitude meditation: Focusing on feelings of gratitude during meditation.

– Gratitude walks: Taking a walk and focusing on things you are grateful for in nature or your surroundings.

– Gratitude rituals: Creating daily or weekly rituals that help you cultivate feelings of gratitude, such as saying a prayer or blessing before meals.

Overcoming Barriers to Gratitude

Despite the many benefits of gratitude, it can be difficult to cultivate in our fast-paced, modern lives. Some common barriers to gratitude include:

– Negativity bias: Our brains are wired to focus on negative experiences, which can make it harder to appreciate the positive things in our lives.

– Comparison: Comparing ourselves to others can lead to feelings of envy and dissatisfaction, making it harder to feel grateful for what we have.

## 13: THE POWER OF GRATITUDE: HOW GRATITUDE ENHANCES JOY

– Busyness: Our busy lives can make it challenging to take the time to reflect on and appreciate the good things in our lives.

To overcome these barriers, it can be helpful to intentionally practice gratitude and make it a part of your daily routine. This might involve setting aside time each day for gratitude practices, or simply taking a few moments throughout the day to reflect on the good things in your life.

Conclusion

Gratitude is a powerful tool for enhancing joy and improving overall well-being. By cultivating gratitude through intentional practices and overcoming common barriers, you can experience greater joy and fulfillment in your life.

# 14: Mindfulness and Joy: Using Mindfulness to Cultivate Joy in Your Life

Introduction:

Mindfulness and joy are two concepts that are closely inter-connected. Mindfulness, which involves paying attention to the present moment with an attitude of openness and non-judgment, can help us to cultivate joy by increasing our awareness of the positive experiences that are already present in our lives. In this chapter, we will explore the relationship between mindfulness and joy, and provide practical strategies for using mindfulness to cultivate greater joy and happiness in your life.

What is Mindfulness?

Before we explore the relationship between mindfulness and joy, it is important to first understand what mindfulness is. Mindfulness is a practice that involves intentionally paying attention to the present moment with an attitude of curiosity, openness, and non-judgment. This means focusing our attention on our thoughts, feelings, and sensations as they arise in the present moment, without getting caught up in them or reacting to them.

How Mindfulness Cultivates Joy

One of the key ways that mindfulness can help us to cultivate joy is by increasing our awareness of the positive experiences that are already present in our lives. Often, we are so focused on the negative aspects of our lives, such as stress, anxiety, and worry, that we fail to notice the many positive experiences that are happening around us. By practicing mindfulness, we can train our minds to notice the good things in our lives and to savor them fully.

For example, imagine that you are walking through a beautiful park on a sunny day. Without mindfulness, you might be so caught up in your thoughts and worries that you fail to notice the beauty of the park around you. However, if you practice mindfulness, you can intentionally focus your attention on the beauty of the trees, the sound of the birds singing, and the warmth of the sun on your skin. By doing so, you can cultivate a sense of joy and appreciation for the beauty of the present moment.

Practical Strategies for Using Mindfulness to Cultivate Joy

## 14: MINDFULNESS AND JOY: USING MINDFULNESS TO CULTIVATE JOY IN YOUR LIFE

There are many practical strategies that you can use to cultivate joy through mindfulness. Some of these strategies include:

– Gratitude practice: Practicing gratitude involves intentionally focusing your attention on the things in your life that you are grateful for. By doing so, you can cultivate a sense of joy and appreciation for the good things that are already present in your life. To practice gratitude, you can start by taking a few moments each day to reflect on the things that you are grateful for, such as your health, your family, your friends, or your job.

– Mindful breathing: Mindful breathing is a simple but powerful mindfulness practice that involves focusing your attention on your breath as it moves in and out of your body. By doing so, you can cultivate a sense of calm and relaxation, which can help to reduce stress and anxiety and increase your capacity for joy. To practice mindful breathing, simply find a quiet place where you can sit comfortably, and focus your attention on your breath as it moves in and out of your body.

– Body scan meditation: Body scan meditation is a mindfulness practice that involves systematically scanning your body from head to toe, paying attention to any sensations or feelings that arise. By doing so, you can increase your awareness of your body and cultivate a sense of joy and appreciation for the sensations and feelings that you experience. To practice body scan meditation, simply lie down in a comfortable position, and systematically scan your body from head to toe, paying attention to any sensations or feelings that arise.

The practice of mindfulness can help individuals cultivate joy by teaching them to observe their thoughts and feelings without becoming attached to them. By doing so, individuals can become more aware of negative patterns of thinking and interrupt them before they spiral out of control. Additionally, mindfulness can help individuals become more present in their daily lives and appreciate the small moments of joy that might have otherwise gone unnoticed.

Incorporating mindfulness practices into daily routines can be done in many ways, such as meditation, deep breathing, or body scans. One popular mindfulness practice is the body scan, where individuals focus their attention on different parts of their body, starting from their toes and moving up to their head. This practice can help individuals become more aware of physical sensations and tune out distractions, leading to a greater sense of relaxation and inner peace.

Another mindfulness practice that can help cultivate joy is gratitude. By taking time to reflect on the things we are grateful for, we can shift our focus away from negative thoughts and towards the positive aspects of our lives. This can help cultivate a sense of joy and contentment, even in the midst of difficult circumstances.

In addition to formal mindfulness practices, individuals can incorporate mindfulness into their daily lives by simply paying more attention to their surroundings and experiences. For example, while eating a meal, individuals can focus on the flavors and textures of the food, rather than mindlessly consuming it while distracted by other things. By doing so, individuals can fully engage with the present moment and experience greater joy and fulfillment.

In conclusion, mindfulness is a powerful tool for cultivating joy in one's life. By becoming more present and aware of their thoughts, feelings, and surroundings, individuals can interrupt negative patterns of thinking and appreciate the small moments of joy that might have otherwise gone unnoticed. By incorporating mindfulness practices into their daily routines, individuals can experience greater levels of happiness and fulfillment, and cultivate a more joyful and meaningful life.

# 15: Joyful Living: Living a Joyful Life with Purpose and Meaning

Living a Joyful Life with Purpose and Meaning

What does it mean to live a joyful life with purpose and meaning? For many people, it's a concept that's difficult to define. However, at its core, it's about living a life that is authentic to who you are and brings you a sense of fulfillment and purpose. When you live a life that is aligned with your values, passions, and goals, you'll naturally experience more joy and happiness.

In this chapter, we'll explore the different elements that contribute to living a joyful life with purpose and meaning. We'll discuss the importance of identifying your values and passions, setting goals, practicing self-care, and cultivating healthy relationships. Additionally, we'll examine how to find purpose and meaning in your career, as well as the significance of giving back to others and your community.

Identifying Your Values and Passions

One of the first steps in living a joyful life with purpose and meaning is to identify your values and passions. When you're clear on what's important to you and what makes you happy, it becomes easier to make decisions that are in alignment with your values and passions. You'll also be more likely to seek out experiences that bring you joy and fulfillment.

Setting Goals

Setting goals is an essential part of living a purposeful life. Goals give you direction and a sense of purpose, as well as something to strive for. When setting goals, it's essential to make sure they align with your values and passions. You'll also want to ensure that they're achievable and realistic, as achieving your goals will give you a sense of accomplishment and contribute to your overall happiness.

Practicing Self-Care

Self-care is crucial for living a joyful life with purpose and meaning. When you prioritize your physical, emotional, and mental well-being, you'll be better equipped to handle the challenges and stressors that come with daily life. Self-care can include activities such as exercise, meditation, spending time in nature, or taking a relaxing bath. Whatever activities bring you joy and help you relax and recharge, prioritize them in your life.

Cultivating Healthy Relationships

Healthy relationships are an essential part of living a joyful life with purpose and meaning. When you surround yourself with positive and supportive people, you'll experience greater happiness and fulfillment. Cultivating healthy relationships involves setting boundaries, communicating effectively, and prioritizing quality time with loved ones.

Finding Purpose and Meaning in Your Career

Finding purpose and meaning in your career is an essential component of living a joyful life with purpose and meaning. When you're doing work that aligns with your values and passions, you'll experience greater fulfillment and joy. To find purpose and meaning in your career, it's essential to reflect on your values and passions and consider how they can be integrated into your work.

Giving Back to Others and Your Community

Giving back to others and your community is another crit-

ical element of living a joyful life with purpose and meaning. When you contribute to something larger than yourself,
you'll experience a sense of purpose and fulfillment. Giving
back can take many forms, including volunteering, donating
to charitable causes, or simply being kind and compassionate to those around you.

In conclusion, living a joyful life with purpose and meaning
involves identifying your values and passions, setting
achievable goals, practicing self-care, cultivating healthy relationships, finding purpose and meaning in your career,
and giving back to others and your community. By incorporating these elements into your life, you'll experience
greater joy, fulfillment, and overall well-being.

# 16: Finding Joy in the Simple Things: Celebrating Life's Small Moments

Introduction:

When we think about joy, we often think about big moments in life - weddings, graduations, job promotions, or vacations. However, joy can also be found in the small moments that make up our daily lives. Taking a walk on a sunny day, enjoying a cup of coffee with a friend, or even just sitting quietly and appreciating the beauty around us can bring us immense joy.

In this chapter, we'll explore the concept of finding joy in the simple things and how it can contribute to a more joyful and fulfilling life.

The Power of Mindfulness:

One of the keys to finding joy in the simple things is to practice mindfulness. Mindfulness is the practice of being present and fully engaged in the current moment, without judgment or distraction. When we practice mindfulness, we are better able to appreciate the small moments of joy that we may otherwise overlook.

One way to practice mindfulness is through meditation. By setting aside time each day to sit quietly and focus on the present moment, we can cultivate a greater sense of awareness and appreciation for the world around us. Additionally, practicing mindfulness throughout the day, by focusing on our breath, noticing our surroundings, or simply taking a few deep breaths, can help us stay present and open to the joys that life has to offer.

The Beauty of Nature:

Nature has a way of bringing us back to the present moment and helping us appreciate the simple things in life. Whether it's taking a hike, going for a swim, or just sitting in a park and watching the world go by, spending time in nature can be a powerful way to connect with our sense of joy and wonder.

When we spend time in nature, we are reminded of the beauty and complexity of the world around us. We may notice the way the sun hits the leaves of a tree, or the way a bird flies gracefully through the sky. These small moments of appreciation can bring us a great deal of joy and help us feel more connected to the world around us.

Finding Joy in Everyday Activities:

Another way to find joy in the simple things is to focus on the everyday activities that make up our lives. When we pay attention to the small things we do each day, we can find joy in even the most mundane tasks.

For example, cooking a meal can be a joyful experience when we take the time to appreciate the colors, textures, and aromas of the food. Cleaning our home can also be a source of joy when we focus on the satisfaction of a job well done, and the feeling of creating a peaceful and orderly environment.

Celebrating Life's Small Moments:

Finally, finding joy in the simple things means taking the time to celebrate the small moments in life. Whether it's a milestone achieved, a goal accomplished, or simply a moment of connection with a loved one, taking the time to acknowledge and appreciate these small moments can bring us a great deal of joy and fulfillment.

One way to celebrate these moments is to keep a gratitude journal. Each day, write down three things you are grateful for, no matter how small. This can help you cultivate a greater sense of appreciation for the world around you and remind you of the many joys that life has to offer.

Conclusion:

Finding joy in the simple things is about cultivating a sense of awareness and appreciation for the world around us. By practicing mindfulness, spending time in nature, finding joy in everyday activities, and celebrating life's small moments, we can create a more joyful and fulfilling life. Remember that joy can be found in even the smallest moments, and that by staying present and open to the world around us, we can experience the transformative power of joy in our lives.

# 17: Joyful Creativity: How Creativity Can Bring Joy and Fulfillment

Creativity is a powerful force that can bring immense joy and fulfillment to our lives. It allows us to express ourselves in unique and meaningful ways, to explore new ideas and perspectives, and to connect with others in profound ways. Whether it's through art, music, writing, or any other creative endeavor, engaging in creative pursuits can unlock a deep wellspring of joy and happiness that can transform every aspect of our lives.

In this chapter, we'll explore the many ways that creativity can bring joy and fulfillment into our lives. We'll discuss the benefits of creative expression, how to cultivate a creative mindset, and the practical steps you can take to bring more creativity into your daily routine. Whether you're an experienced artist or just starting out, this chapter will provide you with the tools and inspiration you need to unlock your creative potential and experience the transformative power of joy.

Benefits of Creative Expression

The benefits of engaging in creative expression are numerous and far-reaching. Research has shown that creativity can have a positive impact on our mental and physical health, our relationships, and our overall well-being. Here are just a few of the ways that creative expression can benefit us:

– Reduced Stress and Anxiety: Engaging in creative activities such as art or music can be a powerful stress-reducer. Creative expression can help us to focus our minds and find a sense of calm, allowing us to let go of our worries and anxieties.

– Improved Emotional Well-being: Creativity can be a powerful tool for processing emotions and expressing our innermost feelings. Whether we're using art to explore our inner world or writing to process our thoughts, creative expression can help us to better understand and manage our emotions.

– Increased Self-esteem: Engaging in creative pursuits can boost our sense of self-worth and confidence. By creating something that is uniquely our own, we can feel a sense of pride and accomplishment that can spill over into other areas of our lives.

– Strengthened Relationships: Creative expression can also help us to connect with others on a deeper level. Whether we're collaborating on a project with friends or sharing our creations with a wider audience, creative pursuits can foster a sense of community and connection that can be incredibly rewarding.

– Improved Cognitive Function: Engaging in creative activities can also improve our cognitive function, including our memory, problem-solving skills, and overall mental agility. Studies have shown that engaging in creative activities can even help to stave off age-related cognitive decline.

Cultivating a Creative Mindset

While some people may feel that creativity is something that comes naturally, the truth is that creativity is a skill that can be cultivated and developed over time. Here are a few tips for cultivating a creative mindset:

– Embrace Curiosity: Creativity is fueled by curiosity, so make a conscious effort to stay curious about the world around you. Ask questions, explore new ideas and perspectives, and seek out experiences that challenge your assumptions.

– Cultivate a Sense of Playfulness: Creativity thrives on playfulness, so try to approach creative pursuits with a sense of lightheartedness and fun. Don't be afraid to experiment and take risks, and remember that there are no "right" or "wrong" ways to be creative.

– Make Time for Creative Pursuits: Creativity requires time and space to flourish, so make a conscious effort to carve out time in your schedule for creative pursuits. Whether it's setting aside a few hours each week for art or music, or simply taking a few minutes each day to write in a journal, making time for creativity is essential.

– Embrace Failure: Creativity involves taking risks and making mistakes, so don't be afraid to fail. Embrace failure as an opportunity to learn and grow, and don't let fear of failure hold you back from exploring new ideas and creative possibilities.

– Practice Mindfulness: Creativity often requires a state of mindfulness, where we are fully present and engaged in the creative process. Practice mindfulness techniques such as meditation or deep breathing to help you get into the creative flow.

– Surround Yourself with Inspiration: Surrounding yourself with sources of inspiration can help to fuel your creativity. Whether it's visiting art galleries, listening to music, or reading books, seek out experiences and sources of inspiration that resonate with you.

Practical Steps for Bringing More Creativity into Your Life

Now that we've explored the benefits of creative expression and the mindset necessary to cultivate creativity, let's take a look at some practical steps you can take to bring more creativity into your daily routine:

– Set Aside Time for Creative Pursuits: As we mentioned earlier, making time for creativity is essential. Set aside time each day or week to engage in a creative pursuit that brings you joy, whether it's painting, writing, or playing music.

– Create a Dedicated Space: Having a dedicated space for creative pursuits can help to make them a regular part of your routine. Whether it's a corner of your living room or a separate studio space, create a space that is conducive to creativity and inspiration.

– Collaborate with Others: Collaborating with others can be a great way to spark creativity and generate new ideas. Consider joining a creative group or seeking out like-minded individuals to collaborate with on a project.

– Take Creative Risks: Don't be afraid to take creative risks and try new things. Whether it's experimenting with a new art technique or trying your hand at a new instrument, taking risks can help to expand your creative horizons.

– Find Inspiration in Everyday Life: Inspiration can come from unexpected places, so try to find creative inspiration in your everyday life. Whether it's the colors of a sunset or the patterns in a piece of architecture, seek out beauty and inspiration in the world around you.

Conclusion

Creativity has the power to bring immense joy and fulfillment into our lives. By embracing a creative mindset, setting aside time for creative pursuits, and taking practical steps to cultivate our creativity, we can unlock a deep well-spring of joy and happiness that can transform every aspect of our lives. Whether we're painting, writing, or playing music, engaging in creative pursuits can help us to connect with ourselves and others on a deeper level, and experience the transformative power of joy.

# 18: Joyful Movement: The Role of Exercise and Movement in Promoting Joy

Introduction

When we think of exercise and movement, we often think of the physical benefits such as weight loss, increased strength, and improved cardiovascular health. However, the benefits of exercise and movement go beyond just physical health. In fact, engaging in regular exercise and movement can play a significant role in promoting joy and happiness in our lives. In this chapter, we will explore the many ways in which joyful movement can enhance our lives, and how to incorporate movement into our daily routine to unlock the transformative power of joy.

The Benefits of Joyful Movement

– Improved Mood: Engaging in joyful movement releases endorphins, which are chemicals in the brain that promote feelings of happiness and well-being. Regular exercise and movement can lead to an overall improvement in mood, reducing symptoms of depression and anxiety.

# 18: JOYFUL MOVEMENT: THE ROLE OF EXERCISE AND MOVEMENT IN PROMOTING JOY

– Increased Energy: Contrary to what you may think, exercise and movement can actually increase your energy levels. Regular physical activity can improve your body's ability to produce and utilize energy, leaving you feeling more energized and less fatigued.

– Improved Sleep: Exercise and movement can also improve the quality of your sleep, leading to better overall health and well-being. Regular exercise has been shown to reduce the amount of time it takes to fall asleep and improve the quality of sleep, leaving you feeling more rested and refreshed.

– Reduced Stress: Engaging in joyful movement can also help to reduce stress levels, as physical activity promotes the release of stress-reducing hormones such as cortisol and adrenaline. Regular exercise can help to improve your ability to cope with stress, leading to a more balanced and joyful life.

– Increased Confidence: Regular exercise and movement can also help to increase feelings of confidence and self-esteem. As you become stronger and more capable, you may feel more confident in your abilities, leading to a greater sense of joy and fulfillment in life.

Incorporating Joyful Movement into Your Life

Now that we've explored the many benefits of joyful movement, let's take a look at some practical steps you can take to incorporate movement into your daily routine:

– Start Small: If you're new to exercise or movement, start small and gradually build up your routine. Begin with simple activities such as walking, stretching, or yoga, and gradually increase the intensity and duration of your workouts.

– Find Activities You Enjoy: Engaging in activities that you enjoy is key to making exercise and movement a regular part of your routine. Whether it's dancing, hiking, or swimming, find activities that bring you joy and make you feel good.

– Make It Social: Exercising with others can be a great way to stay motivated and engaged. Consider joining a fitness class, sports team, or workout group to make exercise a social and enjoyable experience.

## 18: JOYFUL MOVEMENT: THE ROLE OF EXERCISE AND MOVEMENT IN PROMOTING JOY

– Mix It Up: Incorporating a variety of activities into your routine can help to keep things interesting and prevent boredom. Try new activities or switch up your routine to keep your body and mind engaged.

– Set Realistic Goals: Setting realistic goals for yourself can help to keep you motivated and on track. Whether it's running a 5K or doing 20 push-ups, setting achievable goals can help to build confidence and a sense of accomplishment.

Conclusion

Engaging in regular joyful movement is key to promoting overall health, happiness, and fulfillment in life. By incorporating movement into our daily routine and finding activities that bring us joy and fulfillment, we can unlock the transformative power of joy and experience a greater sense of well-being. Whether it's walking, dancing, or lifting weights, find activities that make you feel good and make movement a regular part of your life. The benefits are endless, and the joy and fulfillment that come with it are truly priceless.

# 19: Joyful Spirituality: Exploring the Connection Between Spirituality and Joy

Introduction

Spirituality can mean different things to different people, but at its core, it refers to our search for meaning and purpose in life. Many people find a sense of peace, fulfillment, and joy through spiritual practices and beliefs. In this chapter, we will explore the connection between spirituality and joy, and how to cultivate a joyful spirituality in your life.

The Connection Between Spirituality and Joy

– Connection with Something Greater: Many people find joy and fulfillment in their connection to something greater than themselves, whether it's a higher power, nature, or a sense of universal energy. Feeling connected to something larger than ourselves can bring a sense of purpose and meaning to life, which can lead to greater joy and fulfillment.

– Gratitude and Appreciation: Spiritual practices often involve cultivating a sense of gratitude and appreciation for the present moment, as well as for the blessings in our lives. Focusing on gratitude can shift our perspective towards positivity and joy, even in difficult times.

– Inner Peace and Serenity: Many spiritual practices involve cultivating inner peace and serenity, which can help to reduce stress and anxiety and promote a sense of calm and contentment. This inner peace and serenity can lead to greater joy and fulfillment in life.

– Compassion and Connection with Others: Spiritual practices often involve cultivating compassion and connection with others, which can lead to greater joy and fulfillment in life. Feeling connected to others and experiencing compassion towards them can bring a sense of purpose and meaning to our lives.

Cultivating a Joyful Spirituality

– Explore Your Beliefs: Take the time to explore your beliefs and values, and identify what brings you a sense of connection and purpose. Whether it's through prayer, meditation, or connecting with nature, find spiritual practices that resonate with you and bring you joy and fulfillment.

## 19: JOYFUL SPIRITUALITY: EXPLORING THE CONNECTION BETWEEN SPIRITUALITY AND JOY

– Practice Gratitude: Cultivate a sense of gratitude and appreciation for the present moment and for the blessings in your life. Make gratitude a regular practice by keeping a gratitude journal, expressing gratitude to others, or simply taking a moment to reflect on the things you are thankful for.

– Cultivate Inner Peace: Engage in practices that cultivate inner peace and serenity, such as meditation, yoga, or mindfulness. These practices can help to reduce stress and anxiety and promote a sense of calm and contentment, leading to greater joy and fulfillment in life.

– Connect with Others: Cultivate compassion and connection with others by engaging in acts of kindness, volunteering, or participating in a spiritual community. Feeling connected to others and experiencing compassion towards them can bring a sense of purpose and meaning to our lives.

– Embrace the Present Moment: Spirituality often involves a focus on the present moment and being fully present in the here and now. Embrace the present moment and find joy and fulfillment in the simple pleasures of life, such as spending time with loved ones, enjoying nature, or engaging in creative pursuits.

– Mindful Living: Living mindfully means paying attention to the present moment without judgment. It involves being aware of your thoughts and emotions and how they impact your actions and behavior. Practicing mindful living can help you to stay present, reduce stress, and cultivate a sense of inner peace and joy.

– Rituals and Traditions: Many spiritual practices involve rituals and traditions that can bring a sense of connection and purpose to our lives. Whether it's lighting candles, practicing a daily prayer, or participating in a religious ceremony, rituals and traditions can help us to feel connected to something greater than ourselves and bring joy and fulfillment to our lives.

– Self-Reflection: Engage in self-reflection and self-examination to deepen your understanding of yourself and your spiritual beliefs. Take time to reflect on your values and beliefs, and consider how they shape your life and perspective. Self-reflection can help you to identify areas of your life that bring you joy and fulfillment, as well as areas that may need more attention and growth.

– Seek Support: Connect with others who share your spiritual beliefs and values, or seek the guidance of a spiritual leader or counselor. Talking with others who understand and share your beliefs can provide support and encouragement on your spiritual journey.

Conclusion

Spirituality and joy are intricately connected, as spiritual practices can bring a sense of purpose, meaning, and connection to our lives. Cultivating a joyful spirituality involves exploring your beliefs, practicing gratitude and inner peace, connecting with others, embracing the present moment, living mindfully, engaging in rituals and traditions, self-reflection, and seeking support. By incorporating these practices into your life, you can deepen your spiritual connection and experience greater joy and fulfillment.

# 20: Joyful Giving: The Power of Generosity and Giving to Bring Joy

## Introduction

We all know the feeling of giving something to someone else and seeing the joy it brings them. Whether it's a thoughtful gift or a simple act of kindness, giving can bring us a sense of happiness and fulfillment that is difficult to replicate in any other way. In this chapter, we will explore the connection between giving and joy, and the transformative power of generosity in our lives.

## The Benefits of Giving

When we give to others, we are not only benefitting them but also ourselves. Numerous studies have shown that giving can bring a variety of benefits to our mental and physical health, including:

– Reduced Stress: Giving can help to reduce stress levels and promote a sense of well-being.

– Improved Relationships: Giving can strengthen our relationships with others, as it shows that we care and are invested in their well-being.

– Increased Happiness: Giving has been shown to increase feelings of happiness and joy, as it provides a sense of purpose and meaning in our lives.

– Lowered Blood Pressure: Giving has been linked to lower blood pressure, which can reduce the risk of heart disease and other health problems.

– Enhanced Self-Esteem: Giving can enhance our self-esteem and sense of self-worth, as it allows us to see ourselves as helpful and caring individuals.

Ways to Give Joyfully

Giving doesn't have to involve grand gestures or expensive gifts. There are many ways to give joyfully, no matter your financial situation or time constraints. Some ideas include:

– Acts of Kindness: Small acts of kindness, like holding the door open for someone or leaving a kind note, can make a big difference in someone's day.

– Volunteering: Volunteering your time and skills to a cause or organization that you care about can bring a sense of fulfillment and purpose.

– Donations: Donating to a charity or organization that aligns with your values and beliefs can be a powerful way to give back to your community.

– Gifts: Giving thoughtful gifts to loved ones, friends, or coworkers can bring joy and strengthen relationships.

– Time: Giving your time and attention to others, whether it's listening to a friend in need or spending quality time with family, can be a powerful way to give joyfully.

The Power of Gratitude

Gratitude is an essential component of giving joyfully. When we focus on what we have and express gratitude for the blessings in our lives, we are more likely to experience joy and fulfillment. Gratitude can also inspire us to give back to others, as we recognize the abundance in our lives and the importance of sharing our blessings with others.

Incorporating Gratitude into Your Giving

## 20: JOYFUL GIVING: THE POWER OF GENEROSITY AND GIVING TO BRING JOY

There are many ways to incorporate gratitude into your giving practices, including:

– Reflecting on Your Blessings: Take time to reflect on the blessings in your life and express gratitude for them.

– Mindful Giving: When giving, take a moment to focus on the joy and gratitude that giving brings, rather than the cost or effort involved.

– Gratitude Journaling: Keeping a gratitude journal can help to cultivate a sense of gratitude in your daily life, which can inspire you to give joyfully.

– Thank You Notes: Taking the time to write a thank-you note to someone who has given to you can be a powerful way to express gratitude and inspire joyful giving.

– Sharing Your Gratitude: Share your gratitude with others, whether it's through verbal expressions or acts of kindness, to inspire others to give joyfully.

Conclusion

Giving joyfully is a powerful way to cultivate joy and fulfillment in our lives. Whether through acts of kindness, volunteering, donations, gifts, or time, giving can bring a sense of purpose and meaning to our lives, while also benefitting others. By cultivating a sense of gratitude and incorporating it into our giving practices, we can amplify the joy and fulfillment that giving brings, while also inspiring others to give joyfully. So, take some time to reflect on the blessings in your life and consider ways that you can give joyfully to those around you. You may be surprised at how much joy and fulfillment it brings to your life and the lives of others. Remember, joy is contagious, so let's spread it far and wide through the power of joyful giving!

# 21: Joyful Resilience: How to Bounce Back from Life's Challenges with Joy

Life is full of ups and downs, and we all experience setbacks, disappointments, and challenges at some point. However, it's not the challenges themselves that determine our happiness and fulfillment, but rather how we respond to them. In other words, our resilience in the face of adversity plays a crucial role in our overall well-being. But resilience doesn't have to be a dreary or stressful process. In fact, it can be a joyful one.

In this chapter, we will explore the concept of joyful resilience, and how you can use it to bounce back from life's challenges with a sense of joy and fulfillment.

– Embrace the Challenge

The first step to building joyful resilience is to embrace the challenge. Rather than viewing a setback as a negative experience, try to see it as an opportunity for growth and learning. Every challenge we face is a chance to develop new skills, discover new strengths, and gain a new perspective on life.

## 21: JOYFUL RESILIENCE: HOW TO BOUNCE BACK FROM LIFE'S CHALLENGES WITH JOY

When we approach challenges with an open mind and a willingness to learn, we not only build our resilience, but we also discover joy in the process. Joy can come from the sense of accomplishment we feel when we overcome a challenge, or from the new skills and knowledge we gain along the way.

– Practice Gratitude

Gratitude is a powerful tool for building resilience and finding joy in difficult situations. When we focus on the good things in our lives, even in the midst of a challenge, we cultivate a positive mindset that can help us overcome adversity.

Try practicing gratitude by keeping a gratitude journal, where you write down three things you're grateful for each day. You can also take a few minutes each day to reflect on the things you're thankful for, or express gratitude to others in your life.

– Focus on What You Can Control

When facing a difficult situation, it's easy to feel overwhelmed and powerless. However, focusing on what we can control can help us feel more empowered and resilient.

Identify the things that are within your control in the situation, and focus on taking positive actions in those areas. By taking action, we not only build our resilience, but we also feel a sense of agency and joy in knowing that we're doing everything we can to overcome the challenge.

– Connect with Others

Human connection is a powerful tool for building resilience and finding joy in difficult situations. When we connect with others, we not only gain support and encouragement, but we also feel a sense of belonging and purpose.

Reach out to friends or family members for support, or consider joining a support group or community organization related to the challenge you're facing. Connecting with others who have gone through similar experiences can help you feel less alone, and provide valuable insights and strategies for building resilience.

– Practice Self-Care

## 21: JOYFUL RESILIENCE: HOW TO BOUNCE BACK FROM LIFE'S CHALLENGES WITH JOY

Self-care is an essential part of building resilience and finding joy in difficult situations. When we prioritize our own physical and emotional well-being, we have the energy and strength we need to face challenges head-on.

Make time for activities that bring you joy, such as exercise, meditation, or creative pursuits. Take care of your physical health by getting enough sleep, eating a healthy diet, and seeking medical care when necessary. And don't forget to practice self-compassion, acknowledging that setbacks and challenges are a natural part of life, and treating yourself with kindness and understanding.

In conclusion, building joyful resilience is not just about bouncing back from challenges, but about finding joy and fulfillment in the process. By embracing challenges, practicing gratitude, focusing on what we can control, connecting with others, and practicing self-care, we can build our resilience and find joy in even the most difficult situations. So, the next time you face a challenge, remember that you have the power to overcome it with a sense of joy and fulfillment.

# 22: The Joy of Forgiveness: How Forgiveness Can Bring Healing and Joy

## Introduction

Forgiveness is a complex and challenging topic, but it is also one of the most important aspects of our lives. Forgiving someone who has wronged us can be incredibly difficult, but it is also one of the most transformative experiences we can have. In this chapter, we will explore the power of forgiveness, how it can bring healing and joy into our lives, and how to cultivate forgiveness as a daily practice.

## Understanding Forgiveness

Forgiveness is often misunderstood as an act of weakness or a way of condoning the actions of those who have wronged us. However, forgiveness is actually an act of strength and courage that empowers us to move beyond the pain and hurt caused by the actions of others. Forgiveness is not about forgetting or minimizing the harm caused, but rather about releasing the hold that the hurt and pain have on our lives.

Forgiveness can also be a powerful tool for repairing relationships. When we forgive someone who has wronged us, we open the door to healing and reconciliation, and we create space for trust, love, and connection to grow.

The Benefits of Forgiveness

The benefits of forgiveness are numerous and far-reaching. When we forgive someone who has wronged us, we experience a sense of release and freedom from the pain and hurt caused by the offense. We also experience a greater sense of peace and well-being, as well as improved mental and physical health.

Forgiveness has also been linked to increased resilience and the ability to bounce back from life's challenges. When we are able to forgive those who have wronged us, we are better able to cope with stress and adversity, and we are less likely to become overwhelmed by negative emotions.

How to Cultivate Forgiveness

Cultivating forgiveness is not always easy, but it is possible with practice and dedication. Here are some strategies for cultivating forgiveness in your life:

– Acknowledge the hurt: It's important to acknowledge the pain and hurt caused by the actions of others. This doesn't mean that you have to condone their actions, but it does mean that you need to recognize the impact that their actions had on you.

– Let go of anger and resentment: Holding onto anger and resentment only keeps you trapped in the pain and hurt caused by the offense. Letting go of these negative emotions is an essential step in the process of forgiveness.

– Practice empathy: Try to understand the perspective of the person who wronged you. This doesn't mean that you have to excuse their behavior, but it can help you to see the situation from a different perspective.

– Focus on the present: Forgiveness is about letting go of the past and moving forward. Focus on the present moment and the positive things in your life, rather than dwelling on the past.

– Seek support: Forgiveness can be a challenging process,

and it can be helpful to seek support from friends, family, or a mental health professional.

Conclusion

Forgiveness is a powerful tool for bringing healing and joy into our lives. It is not always easy, but with practice and dedication, it is possible to cultivate forgiveness as a daily practice. By acknowledging the hurt, letting go of anger and resentment, practicing empathy, focusing on the present, and seeking support, we can experience the transformative power of forgiveness in our lives.

# 23: Joyful Aging: Embracing Joy and Fulfillment in the Golden Years

Introduction:

Aging is a natural process that every living being goes through. However, in modern society, aging is often associated with negative stereotypes and fear. Many people believe that aging is a time of decline, loss, and unhappiness. However, this is far from the truth. Aging can be a time of great joy, fulfillment, and personal growth. In this chapter, we will explore how to embrace joy and fulfillment in the golden years.

– Embracing Change:

One of the keys to finding joy and fulfillment in the golden years is to embrace change. Aging brings with it many changes, both physical and emotional. However, instead of resisting these changes, we can learn to embrace them. This means accepting that our bodies and minds are changing and finding new ways to engage with the world around us. For example, if we find it difficult to engage in physical activities that we used to enjoy, we can explore new hobbies or interests that we may not have had time for before.

– Cultivating Social Connections:

As we age, social connections become even more important. Research has shown that older adults who maintain strong social connections have better mental and physical health and are more likely to live longer. Therefore, it is important to cultivate social connections with family, friends, and the community. This can include joining clubs or groups that share common interests, volunteering, or participating in community events.

– Staying Active:

Staying physically active is another key to finding joy and fulfillment in the golden years. Physical activity not only improves our physical health but also helps to boost our mood and cognitive function. It is never too late to start an exercise routine, and there are many options available for older adults, such as yoga, swimming, or walking.

– Finding Meaning and Purpose:

As we age, it can be easy to lose a sense of meaning and purpose. However, finding meaning and purpose is important for our mental health and wellbeing. This can include pursuing a passion or interest, volunteering, or even starting a new business or project. By finding something that we are passionate about, we can maintain a sense of purpose and fulfillment in our lives.

– Cultivating Gratitude:

Gratitude is another important component of finding joy and fulfillment in the golden years. By focusing on what we are grateful for, we can shift our perspective to one of positivity and abundance. This can be as simple as keeping a gratitude journal or taking a few moments each day to reflect on what we are thankful for.

– Taking Care of Our Mental Health:

Taking care of our mental health is important at any age, but it becomes even more important as we age. This can include seeking professional help if needed, practicing stress management techniques such as meditation or deep breathing, or engaging in activities that bring us joy and relaxation.

## 23: JOYFUL AGING: EMBRACING JOY AND FULFILL-
## MENT IN THE GOLDEN YEARS

– Embracing the Aging Process:

Finally, one of the most important steps to finding joy and fulfillment in the golden years is to embrace the aging process itself. This means accepting that our bodies and minds will change as we age and that this is a natural part of life. By embracing the aging process, we can learn to appreciate the wisdom and experience that comes with age and focus on living a life of joy and fulfillment.

Conclusion:

Aging is a natural process that can be filled with joy and fulfillment. By embracing change, cultivating social connections, staying active, finding meaning and purpose, cultivating gratitude, taking care of our mental health, and embracing the aging process, we can find joy and fulfillment in the golden years. It is never too late to start living a life of joy and fulfillment, and the golden years can be a time of great growth and personal transformation.

# 24: Joyful Eating: How to Nourish Your Body and Soul with Joyful Foods

Introduction

We all know the saying, "you are what you eat." But have you ever considered that what you eat can also affect your mood and overall well-being? Eating well doesn't just fuel your body with the necessary nutrients, it can also bring joy and satisfaction to your life. This chapter explores the connection between food and joy, and offers tips for how to embrace joyful eating in your daily life.

The Joyful Eating Mindset

Joyful eating is about more than just the food on your plate. It's also about the mindset you bring to your meals. When you approach eating with a sense of joy and appreciation, it can elevate the entire experience. Here are a few ways to cultivate a joyful eating mindset:

– Practice gratitude: Before you take your first bite, take a moment to express gratitude for the food in front of you. Consider the effort and resources that went into producing and preparing it. This simple act can bring a sense of appreciation and joy to your meal.

– Slow down and savor: Instead of rushing through your meals, take the time to savor each bite. Pay attention to the flavors, textures, and aromas of the food. Eating mindfully can help you feel more present and connected to your food, which can lead to greater joy and satisfaction.

– Release guilt and shame: Eating should never be a source of guilt or shame. Instead of beating yourself up for indulging in your favorite treats or skipping a workout, practice self-compassion and move on. Joyful eating is about finding balance and pleasure in food without judgment.

Joyful Foods

Certain foods have been shown to promote joy and well-being. Here are a few examples:

– Fruits and vegetables: A diet rich in fruits and vegetables has been linked to lower rates of depression and greater overall well-being. These foods are packed with vitamins, minerals, and antioxidants that can support a healthy body and mind.

– Whole grains: Whole grains are a good source of fiber, which can promote feelings of fullness and satiety. This can help prevent overeating and promote stable blood sugar levels, which can contribute to a more balanced mood.

– Healthy fats: Foods like avocados, nuts, and fatty fish are rich in healthy fats like omega-3s, which have been shown to reduce inflammation and improve brain function. These fats can also help improve mood and promote feelings of well-being.

Joyful Eating in Practice

Embracing joyful eating doesn't have to be complicated or restrictive. Here are a few tips for incorporating joy and satisfaction into your meals:

– Make mealtime special: Eating is a daily occurrence, but that doesn't mean it has to be mundane. Try setting the table with your favorite dishes and lighting a candle to create a special atmosphere. You can also invite friends or family to join you for a shared meal, which can bring a sense of community and joy to the experience.

– Cook with joy: Cooking can be a source of stress or frustration for some, but it can also be an opportunity for creativity and joy. Experiment with new recipes or try cooking your favorite meals from scratch. You can also listen to music or enjoy a glass of wine while you cook to make the experience more enjoyable.

– Indulge mindfully: There's nothing wrong with enjoying your favorite treats from time to time. However, it's important to do so mindfully. Rather than mindlessly snacking on junk food, savor a small portion of your favorite treat and enjoy it fully.

Another way to incorporate joy into your eating habits is to make mealtime a social event. Sharing meals with loved ones or friends can be a source of great joy and fulfillment. Plan a weekly dinner party, organize a potluck with friends, or simply invite a neighbor over for a meal. Eating with others can create a sense of community and belonging, and can be an opportunity to share in the joy of good food and good company.

Additionally, practicing mindfulness while eating can enhance the joy and pleasure of your food. Mindful eating involves paying attention to the textures, flavors, and smells of your food, as well as being present in the moment and savoring each bite. This can be a simple but powerful practice that can bring greater joy and satisfaction to your eating experience.

It's also important to acknowledge the joy that food can bring beyond just its nutritional value. Food can be a source of cultural connection, as well as a way to celebrate special occasions and traditions. Whether it's a favorite childhood recipe or a dish enjoyed during holidays or festivals, food can be a way to connect to your roots and bring joy and meaning to your life.

In addition to these tips, there are also certain foods that are known to boost mood and promote joy. These include foods rich in omega-3 fatty acids, such as fatty fish like salmon or nuts and seeds, which have been shown to have antidepressant effects. Foods high in tryptophan, like turkey and bananas, can also promote the production of serotonin, a neurotransmitter linked to mood and happiness.

# 24: JOYFUL EATING: HOW TO NOURISH YOUR BODY AND SOUL WITH JOYFUL FOODS

In conclusion, eating with joy is about more than just choosing healthy foods or avoiding unhealthy ones. It's about developing a positive relationship with food, one that emphasizes pleasure, mindfulness, and connection. By incorporating these practices into your eating habits, you can experience greater joy and fulfillment in your daily life.

# 25: Joyful Sleep: How Good Sleep Can Enhance Your Joy and Well-Being

Introduction:

Sleep is essential for our physical, mental, and emotional health. However, in today's fast-paced world, many people struggle to get enough quality sleep. Poor sleep can lead to a host of health problems, including depression, anxiety, obesity, heart disease, and more. It can also impact our overall sense of joy and well-being. In this chapter, we will explore the connection between sleep and joy and provide practical tips on how to get better sleep.

The Science of Sleep:

To understand how sleep impacts our joy and well-being, it's important to first understand the science of sleep. When we sleep, our bodies go through several stages of sleep, including light sleep, deep sleep, and REM (rapid eye movement) sleep. Each stage plays a crucial role in our physical and mental health.

During deep sleep, our bodies repair and regenerate cells,

while our brains consolidate memories and process emotions. REM sleep, on the other hand, is when we dream and process emotions on a deeper level. Lack of sleep or poor sleep quality can disrupt these crucial processes and leave us feeling tired, moody, and less joyful.

The Connection Between Sleep and Joy:

Getting enough quality sleep is essential for our overall sense of joy and well-being. When we are well-rested, we are more likely to have a positive outlook on life, be more productive, and have more energy to pursue our passions and hobbies. On the other hand, lack of sleep can lead to negative emotions like irritability, anxiety, and depression.

Sleep also plays a crucial role in our relationships. When we are well-rested, we are better able to communicate and connect with others. We are also more patient and understanding, which can lead to deeper, more meaningful relationships.

Tips for Better Sleep:

If you're struggling to get enough quality sleep, there are

several things you can do to improve your sleep habits:

– Stick to a regular sleep schedule: Try to go to bed and wake up at the same time every day, even on weekends.

– Create a relaxing sleep environment: Make sure your bedroom is cool, dark, and quiet. Use comfortable bedding and invest in a good mattress and pillows.

– Limit screen time before bed: The blue light emitted by electronic devices can disrupt sleep. Try to avoid using screens for at least an hour before bed.

– Avoid caffeine and alcohol: Both can disrupt sleep quality, so it's best to avoid them in the hours leading up to bedtime.

– Practice relaxation techniques: Meditation, deep breathing, and yoga can all help you relax and prepare for sleep.

– Get regular exercise: Regular exercise can help you sleep better, but try to avoid exercising too close to bedtime.

– Seek professional help: If you've tried these tips and still have trouble sleeping, it may be time to seek help from a medical professional.

Conclusion:

Getting enough quality sleep is essential for our physical, mental, and emotional health. It's also a crucial component of our overall sense of joy and well-being. By prioritizing sleep and following the tips outlined in this chapter, you can improve your sleep habits and experience more joy in your life.

# 26: Joyful Travel: How Travel Can Bring Joy and Adventure to Your Life

Introduction

Traveling is an activity that can bring joy and adventure to our lives. It can provide us with new experiences, opportunities to learn, and moments of reflection. In this chapter, we will explore the ways in which travel can bring joy and fulfillment to our lives, and how we can make the most of our travels to enhance our well-being.

The Benefits of Travel

Traveling offers a wealth of benefits that can contribute to our overall happiness and well-being. These benefits include:

– Exposure to new cultures and experiences. Traveling allows us to experience new cultures, foods, languages, and ways of life. This exposure can broaden our perspective and help us to appreciate the diversity of the world.

– Opportunities for personal growth. Traveling can challenge us to step outside of our comfort zones, try new things, and develop new skills. It can also provide us with opportunities for self-reflection and personal growth.

– Relaxation and stress relief. Traveling can provide us with a much-needed break from the stresses of daily life. It can allow us to disconnect from work and other responsibilities, and to focus on rest and relaxation.

– Connection with others. Traveling can provide opportunities to connect with people from different backgrounds and cultures. These connections can enrich our lives and provide us with new perspectives.

– Creation of lasting memories. Traveling can create memories that last a lifetime. These memories can bring us joy and provide us with a sense of nostalgia in the future.

Making the Most of Your Travel Experience

To make the most of your travel experience, it's important to approach your trip with an open mind and a positive attitude. Here are some tips for maximizing the joy and fulfillment you get from your travels:

– Plan ahead, but be flexible. While it's important to have a general plan for your trip, it's also important to be flexible and open to new experiences. Leave some room in your itinerary for spontaneity and unexpected discoveries.

– Embrace the local culture. Immerse yourself in the local culture by trying local foods, attending local events, and learning about the history and traditions of the place you're visiting.

– Connect with locals. Strike up conversations with locals and learn from them. They can provide valuable insight into the culture and help you to experience the place in a more authentic way.

– Step outside of your comfort zone. Push yourself to try new things, even if they make you feel uncomfortable at first. This could be anything from trying a new food to participating in an adventurous activity.

– Take time to reflect. While it's important to be present and enjoy your travels, it's also important to take time to reflect on the experiences you're having. Take time each day to journal, meditate, or simply sit quietly and observe the world around you.

Conclusion

Traveling can be a powerful tool for bringing joy and adventure to our lives. By embracing the local culture, connecting with locals, and stepping outside of our comfort zones, we can make the most of our travel experiences and enhance our overall well-being. Whether we're exploring a new city or venturing to a far-off land, travel can provide us with a sense of wonder and discovery that can bring joy to our lives for years to come.

# 27: Joyful Minimalism: Simplifying Your Life for Greater Joy and Fulfillment

Introduction:

In a world that glorifies excess and consumerism, the concept of minimalism has gained a lot of popularity in recent years. Minimalism is the practice of intentionally living with fewer material possessions, focusing on what's essential, and letting go of the excess. While minimalism is often associated with decluttering physical space, it can also be applied to various areas of our lives, including our schedule, relationships, and digital presence. In this chapter, we will explore the connection between minimalism and joy, and how simplifying your life can lead to greater happiness and fulfillment.

The Connection Between Minimalism and Joy:

At its core, minimalism is about focusing on what truly matters and letting go of what doesn't. By reducing the clutter and noise in our lives, we create more space for the things that bring us joy and fulfillment. This can mean different things for different people, but in general, minimalism helps us to:

— Live in the present moment: When we have fewer distractions and obligations, we can be more present and mindful in our daily lives. This allows us to fully enjoy the simple pleasures and joys of life that we might otherwise overlook.

— Cultivate gratitude: By simplifying our lives, we learn to appreciate what we have rather than always striving for more. This cultivates a sense of gratitude and contentment that can lead to greater joy and fulfillment.

— Build meaningful relationships: When we focus on quality over quantity, we can invest more time and energy into building deep and meaningful relationships with the people we care about. This connection can bring us immense joy and support throughout our lives.

— Pursue our passions: By letting go of the excess, we create more time and space for the things that truly matter to us. This can mean pursuing a hobby, starting a new project, or pursuing a long-held dream. When we are able to focus on our passions, we feel a sense of purpose and fulfillment that can bring us great joy.

## 27: JOYFUL MINIMALISM: SIMPLIFYING YOUR LIFE FOR GREATER JOY AND FULFILLMENT

How to Embrace Minimalism for Greater Joy and Fulfillment:

– Start with your physical space: Decluttering your physical space can be a powerful first step in embracing minimalism. Start by identifying the items that bring you joy and the ones that don't. Let go of the excess and create a space that feels clean, calm, and intentional.

– Simplify your schedule: Just as our physical space can become cluttered, so can our schedule. Learn to say no to obligations that don't bring you joy or that are not essential. Create space in your schedule for the things that truly matter to you.

– Cultivate gratitude: Make a conscious effort to appreciate what you have rather than focusing on what you don't. Practice gratitude daily by writing down three things you are thankful for each day.

– Build meaningful relationships: Invest time and energy into building deep and meaningful relationships with the people you care about. This might mean scheduling regular date nights with your partner, calling your parents once a week, or making time for a long-distance friend.

– Pursue your passions: Identify the things that truly matter to you and make time for them. Whether it's pursuing a hobby, starting a new project, or taking a class, make space in your life for the things that bring you joy and fulfillment.

Conclusion:

Minimalism is a powerful tool for creating greater joy and fulfillment in our lives. By intentionally simplifying our lives, we create space for the things that truly matter and let go of the excess that can weigh us down. Whether you start with your physical space or your schedule, the key is to focus on what truly matters and let go of the rest. By embracing minimalism, you can create a life filled with joy, purpose, and fulfillment.

# 28: Joyful Entrepreneurship: How to Build a Business That Brings Joy and Purpose

Introduction

Entrepreneurship can be a challenging and rewarding experience. Starting and running a business can be a daunting task, but it can also bring a great sense of accomplishment and purpose. Joyful entrepreneurship involves building a business that not only provides financial success but also brings joy and fulfillment. This chapter will explore the connection between entrepreneurship and joy, the benefits of joyful entrepreneurship, and practical tips for building a business that brings joy and purpose.

The Connection Between Entrepreneurship and Joy

Entrepreneurship can be a source of joy and fulfillment for many reasons. For one, it allows individuals to pursue their passions and turn them into a viable business. When individuals are able to create a business based on their passions and interests, it can bring a sense of purpose and meaning to their work. Moreover, entrepreneurs have the ability to create something from scratch, which can be a rewarding experience in and of itself.

Additionally, entrepreneurship allows individuals to have greater control over their work-life balance. Entrepreneurs have the flexibility to set their own schedules and work on their own terms, which can help to reduce stress and increase overall well-being. They also have the ability to create a company culture that aligns with their values and beliefs, which can be a source of joy and fulfillment.

Benefits of Joyful Entrepreneurship

Joyful entrepreneurship has numerous benefits, including:

– Increased job satisfaction: When individuals are able to build a business that aligns with their passions and values, it can bring a greater sense of fulfillment and job satisfaction.

– Improved mental health: Joyful entrepreneurship can also have a positive impact on mental health. By pursuing work that brings joy and fulfillment, individuals may experience less stress, anxiety, and burnout.

– Increased creativity and innovation: Joyful entrepreneurs

are often more creative and innovative in their work because they are motivated by their passions and interests.

– Greater financial success: Building a business that brings joy and purpose can also lead to greater financial success because individuals are more likely to put in the time and effort required to make their business successful.

– Positive impact on society: Joyful entrepreneurship can also have a positive impact on society. When individuals are able to build a business that aligns with their values and beliefs, they are more likely to make decisions that benefit society as a whole.

Practical Tips for Joyful Entrepreneurship

Here are some practical tips for building a business that brings joy and purpose:

– Identify your passions and interests: The first step in building a joyful business is to identify your passions and interests. Ask yourself what you enjoy doing, what brings you joy, and what you are most passionate about.

– Create a mission statement: Once you have identified

your passions and interests, create a mission statement that
reflects your values and goals. This will help to guide your
business decisions and ensure that your work aligns with
your values.

– Build a team that shares your values: As you build your
business, it is important to surround yourself with people
who share your values and beliefs. This will help to create a
positive company culture and ensure that everyone is working towards the same goals.

– Focus on creating value: One of the keys to building a successful business is to focus on creating value for your customers. When you are able to provide value and solve problems for your customers, your business will be more likely
to succeed.

– Stay adaptable and flexible: Building a business can be
unpredictable, so it is important to stay adaptable and flexible. Be open to new ideas and be willing to pivot your business model if necessary.

– Embrace failure: Failure is a natural part of entrepreneurship, so it is important to embrace it and learn from it.

## 28: JOYFUL ENTREPRENEURSHIP: HOW TO BUILD A BUSINESS THAT BRINGS JOY AND PURPOSE

Rather than viewing failure as a negative experience, see it as an opportunity to learn and grow.

Harness the Power of Community

Entrepreneurship can be a lonely road, but it doesn't have to be. Building a community around your business can be incredibly rewarding and bring a sense of joy and purpose to your work.

This can be done in a number of ways. You can start by connecting with other entrepreneurs in your industry or niche, either in person or online. Attend networking events, join online groups, and participate in forums and discussions related to your field.

You can also build a community around your brand by engaging with your customers and followers on social media. Respond to comments, share user-generated content, and create a sense of community and belonging around your brand.

Finally, consider collaborating with other entrepreneurs or businesses in your community. This can help you expand your reach and build meaningful relationships with like-minded individuals.

### Focus on Your Why

As an entrepreneur, it's important to have a clear sense of purpose and passion for what you do. This sense of purpose is often referred to as your "why," and it can be a powerful motivator and source of joy.

Take some time to reflect on your why. What inspired you to start your business in the first place? What impact do you hope to have on the world? How does your business align with your values and passions?

By focusing on your why, you can stay connected to your sense of purpose and motivation, even during challenging times. This can bring a sense of joy and fulfillment to your work, as you feel that you are making a meaningful difference in the world.

### Embrace Learning and Growth

Finally, remember that entrepreneurship is a journey of learning and growth. Embrace this journey and commit to ongoing personal and professional development.

Invest in courses, workshops, and coaching to help you improve your skills and knowledge. Seek out mentors and advisors who can provide guidance and support. And stay open to feedback and new ideas, even if they challenge your assumptions or comfort zone.

By committing to learning and growth, you can continually improve your business and yourself, bringing a sense of joy and satisfaction to your work.

Conclusion

Entrepreneurship can be a challenging and rewarding path, but it's important to remember that joy and fulfillment are possible, even in the midst of hard work and uncertainty.

By embracing a joyful mindset, building a supportive community, staying connected to your sense of purpose, and committing to ongoing learning and growth, you can build a business that brings joy and fulfillment to your life and the lives of others.

# 29: Joyful Creativity: How to Unlock Your Creative Potential for Greater Joy

Introduction

Creativity is not just limited to the realm of artists and writers. Everyone has the potential to be creative, and engaging in creative pursuits can bring joy and fulfillment to our lives. In this chapter, we will explore how to unlock your creative potential and use it to experience more joy in your life.

The Benefits of Creativity

Creativity is a powerful tool that can bring many benefits to our lives. Engaging in creative pursuits can help us to:

– Reduce stress and anxiety

– Improve mood and emotional wellbeing

– Increase self-confidence and self-esteem

– Enhance problem-solving skills

## 29: JOYFUL CREATIVITY: HOW TO UNLOCK YOUR CREATIVE POTENTIAL FOR GREATER JOY

– Foster a sense of purpose and meaning

– Boost brain function and cognitive abilities

Unlocking Your Creative Potential

While some people seem to be born with a natural talent for creativity, the truth is that anyone can become more creative with practice and effort. Here are some tips for unlocking your creative potential:

– Give yourself permission to be creative. Many people hold themselves back from pursuing creative endeavors because they feel they are not talented enough or fear failure. However, creativity is not about being perfect or creating a masterpiece. It's about the process of exploring and experimenting. Give yourself permission to make mistakes and have fun with the creative process.

– Cultivate curiosity. Being curious and open-minded can help you see things from a new perspective and spark creative ideas. Take time to explore new interests, learn new skills, and try new things.

– Embrace your uniqueness. Your personal experiences,

perspectives, and quirks can all contribute to your creative output. Don't be afraid to express your unique voice and style in your creative pursuits.

– Practice regularly. Like any skill, creativity requires practice to develop. Set aside time each day or week to engage in creative activities, whether it's writing, painting, or playing an instrument.

– Collaborate with others. Working with others can inspire new ideas and bring fresh perspectives to your creative process. Consider joining a creative group or partnering with a friend on a project.

Using Creativity to Find Joy

Now that you've unlocked your creative potential, how can you use it to experience more joy in your life? Here are some ideas:

– Create for yourself. Don't worry about creating something for an audience or trying to impress others. Focus on creating something that brings you joy and fulfillment.

– Use creativity to express your emotions. Creative pursuits can be a powerful way to process and express emotions. Consider writing in a journal, creating art, or composing music to work through difficult emotions.

– Share your creativity with others. Sharing your creative work with others can bring a sense of connection and community. Consider sharing your work on social media, participating in a local art show, or hosting a writing workshop.

– Use creativity to enhance your surroundings. Creating a beautiful and inspiring environment can bring joy to your daily life. Consider adding art, plants, or other decorative elements to your home or workspace.

Conclusion

Creativity is a powerful tool for bringing joy and fulfillment to our lives. By unlocking your creative potential and engaging in creative pursuits, you can experience the many benefits that creativity has to offer. Use creativity to express yourself, process emotions, connect with others, and enhance your surroundings, and watch as joy and fulfillment fill your life.

# 30: Joyful Mindset: How to Cultivate a Positive Mindset for Lasting Joy

The power of the mind is an incredible thing. Our thoughts have the ability to shape our emotions, actions, and ultimately our lives. Cultivating a positive mindset is one of the most important steps we can take towards experiencing lasting joy and fulfillment in every aspect of our lives.

In this chapter, we will explore the concept of a joyful mindset, including the benefits of positive thinking, the challenges of maintaining a positive outlook, and practical strategies for cultivating a joyful mindset that can lead to a happier, more fulfilling life.

Benefits of a Positive Mindset

A positive mindset is associated with numerous benefits, including improved mental and physical health, increased resilience, enhanced creativity, and better relationships. Positive thinking has been linked to lower levels of stress and anxiety, improved immune function, and a reduced risk of depression and other mental health issues.

## 30: JOYFUL MINDSET: HOW TO CULTIVATE A POSITIVE MINDSET FOR LASTING JOY

When we approach life with a positive mindset, we are more likely to experience joy and happiness, even in the face of adversity. A positive outlook can help us navigate challenging situations, overcome obstacles, and find meaning and purpose in our lives.

Challenges of Maintaining a Positive Outlook

While a positive mindset can be incredibly beneficial, it is not always easy to maintain. Life is full of challenges and setbacks that can test even the most positive of attitudes. We may face difficult circumstances, such as illness, loss, or financial hardship, that make it challenging to stay optimistic.

In addition, our brains are wired to focus on negative experiences, which can make it difficult to maintain a positive mindset. This negativity bias is a survival mechanism that helped our ancestors avoid danger, but in today's world, it can lead to rumination and anxiety.

Practical Strategies for Cultivating a Joyful Mindset

Despite these challenges, it is possible to cultivate a joyful mindset through intentional practice and self-awareness. Here are some practical strategies that can help:

– Practice gratitude: Cultivate a daily gratitude practice by taking time to reflect on the things in your life that you are thankful for. This can help shift your focus towards the positive and increase your sense of wellbeing.

– Reframe negative thoughts: When you notice yourself thinking negatively, try reframing your thoughts in a more positive light. For example, instead of thinking "I'll never be able to do this," try thinking "I haven't figured it out yet, but I'm making progress."

– Focus on solutions: When faced with a challenge, try to focus on finding solutions rather than dwelling on the problem. This can help you feel more empowered and in control of your situation.

– Surround yourself with positivity: Surround yourself with positive people, experiences, and environments as much as possible. Seek out activities that bring you joy and spend time with people who lift you up.

## 30: JOYFUL MINDSET: HOW TO CULTIVATE A POSITIVE MINDSET FOR LASTING JOY

— Practice self-compassion: Be kind and compassionate to yourself, especially when things don't go as planned. Treat yourself with the same love and respect that you would offer to a close friend.

— Practice mindfulness: Practice mindfulness techniques, such as meditation, to help quiet your mind and focus on the present moment. This can help reduce stress and increase feelings of wellbeing.

— Cultivate a growth mindset: Embrace a growth mindset, which involves believing that your abilities and intelligence can be developed through hard work and dedication. This can help you approach challenges with a sense of curiosity and optimism, rather than fear and self-doubt.

Conclusion

Cultivating a joyful mindset is a powerful way to experience greater happiness and fulfillment in every aspect of your life. While it may not always be easy, with intentional practice and self-awareness, it is possible to shift your mindset towards the positive and experience the transformative power of joy. By practicing gratitude, reframing negative thoughts, focusing on solutions, surrounding yourself with positivity, practicing self-compassion

# 31: Joyful Boundaries: Setting Boundaries to Protect Your Joy and Well-Being

As social creatures, humans naturally seek connection and relationships with others. However, without appropriate boundaries, relationships can become toxic, draining, and detrimental to our well-being. In this chapter, we will explore the concept of joyful boundaries, including why they are important, how to set them, and the benefits of having healthy boundaries in our lives.

What are Boundaries?

Boundaries are the limits we set for ourselves in our relationships with others. They are the guidelines that help us protect our physical, emotional, and mental well-being. Boundaries help us define what we are comfortable with and what we are not, and they help us communicate our needs to others.

Why are Boundaries Important?

Boundaries are essential for our well-being and the health of our relationships. Without boundaries, we may find

ourselves constantly giving to others without receiving anything in return, or we may become enmeshed in toxic or
codependent relationships.

When we set and enforce healthy boundaries, we are better
able to:

– Protect our physical, emotional, and mental health

– Establish and maintain healthy relationships

– Preserve our self-respect and dignity

– Feel more in control of our lives and decisions

– Experience greater joy and fulfillment

How to Set Boundaries

Setting boundaries can be challenging, especially if we are
not used to asserting our needs or if we fear rejection or
conflict. However, with practice, it becomes easier to set
and enforce healthy boundaries. Here are some steps you
can take to establish joyful boundaries:

– Identify your needs: Start by identifying your needs and

what is important to you. What are your values and beliefs? What makes you feel happy and fulfilled? This will help you identify what boundaries you need to set.

– Communicate clearly: Be clear and direct when communicating your boundaries to others. Use "I" statements to express how you feel and what you need. For example, "I feel uncomfortable when you criticize me in front of others. I need you to talk to me privately if you have concerns."

– Be consistent: Once you set a boundary, be consistent in enforcing it. This shows others that you are serious about your needs and that you respect yourself enough to uphold your boundaries.

– Practice self-care: Setting boundaries can be emotionally taxing, so it's important to practice self-care. Take time to do things that make you feel good, such as exercise, spending time with loved ones, or practicing mindfulness techniques.

– Seek support: If you are struggling to set or enforce boundaries, seek support from a therapist, trusted friend, or support group. They can provide you with guidance, encouragement, and feedback.

Benefits of Healthy Boundaries

Having healthy boundaries in our lives can lead to numerous benefits, including:

– Greater self-esteem and self-worth

– Increased emotional resilience and mental health

– More fulfilling and satisfying relationships

– Reduced stress and anxiety

– Greater sense of control over our lives and decisions

Conclusion

Setting and enforcing joyful boundaries is an essential step in protecting our well-being and experiencing lasting joy and fulfillment in our lives. By identifying our needs, communicating clearly, being consistent, practicing self-care, and seeking support, we can establish healthy boundaries that help us cultivate positive relationships and lead happier, more fulfilling lives. Remember, setting boundaries is

## 31: JOYFUL BOUNDARIES: SETTING BOUNDARIES TO PROTECT YOUR JOY AND WELL-BEING

not selfish, it is a necessary act of self-care and self-respect.

# 32: Joyful Acceptance: Learning to Accept Life's Challenges with Joy

Life is full of ups and downs, highs and lows, and unexpected twists and turns. No matter how hard we try to control our lives, we cannot control everything that happens to us. However, we can control how we respond to the challenges that life throws our way. In this chapter, we will explore the concept of joyful acceptance, including what it means, why it is important, and how to cultivate it in our lives.

What is Joyful Acceptance?

Joyful acceptance is the ability to accept life's challenges and setbacks with a positive, open-minded attitude. It is about embracing life's imperfections and uncertainties, rather than resisting or fighting against them. Joyful acceptance allows us to let go of our need for control and perfectionism, and instead embrace the present moment with a sense of gratitude and joy.

Why is Joyful Acceptance Important?

Joyful acceptance is important for our well-being and happiness because it allows us to:

– Reduce stress and anxiety: When we resist or fight against the challenges of life, we can create more stress and anxiety for ourselves. Joyful acceptance helps us to release this tension and find peace in the present moment.

– Increase resilience: Accepting challenges with a positive attitude helps us to bounce back from setbacks and adapt to change more easily.

– Cultivate gratitude: By accepting life's challenges, we can develop a greater sense of gratitude for the good things in our lives.

– Experience more joy: When we accept life's challenges with joy, we can find meaning and purpose in even the most difficult situations.

How to Cultivate Joyful Acceptance

Cultivating joyful acceptance requires practice and patience, but the benefits are well worth the effort. Here are some steps you can take to cultivate joyful acceptance in your life:

## 32: JOYFUL ACCEPTANCE: LEARNING TO ACCEPT LIFE'S CHALLENGES WITH JOY

Practice mindfulness: Mindfulness is the practice of being present and non-judgmental in the moment. By practicing mindfulness, we can learn to accept our thoughts and emotions without resistance, and find peace in the present moment.

Let go of control: Accepting life's challenges requires letting go of our need for control and perfectionism. Practice letting go of the things that are outside of your control and focus on what you can control.

Embrace imperfection: Nobody is perfect, and life is full of imperfections. Embrace your own imperfections and accept the imperfections of others.

Focus on the positive: Even in the midst of challenges, there is always something positive to focus on. Practice gratitude and focus on the good things in your life.

Seek support: It's okay to ask for help when we are struggling to accept life's challenges. Seek support from friends, family, or a therapist to help you cultivate a more positive and accepting mindset.

# 32: JOYFUL ACCEPTANCE: LEARNING TO ACCEPT LIFE'S CHALLENGES WITH JOY

Benefits of Joyful Acceptance

Cultivating joyful acceptance in our lives can lead to numerous benefits, including:

– Increased resilience and adaptability

– Greater sense of peace and calm

– Enhanced relationships with others

– Greater sense of purpose and meaning

– More joy and happiness in everyday life

Conclusion

Joyful acceptance is about learning to accept life's challenges with a positive and open-minded attitude. By practicing mindfulness, letting go of control, embracing imperfection, focusing on the positive, and seeking support, we can cultivate a more joyful and accepting mindset. Remember, life is full of challenges, but how we choose to respond to them is within our control. Choose joy and acceptance, and experience a more fulfilling and joyful life.

# 33: Joyful Community: Building and Sustaining a Joyful Community

Humans are social creatures, and we thrive in communities. When we feel connected to others and have a sense of belonging, we experience greater happiness and well-being. In this chapter, we will explore the concept of joyful community, including what it means, why it is important, and how to build and sustain a joyful community in your life.

What is Joyful Community?

Joyful community refers to a group of individuals who share a sense of connection, purpose, and joy. It is a community where members feel seen, heard, and supported, and where they can contribute to something greater than themselves. Joyful community can take many forms, from a close-knit group of friends to a larger community organization.

Why is Joyful Community Important?

Joyful community is important for our well-being and happiness because it allows us to:

Feel connected and supported: When we feel connected to others, we feel less alone and more supported in our lives.

Develop a sense of purpose: Being part of a community can give us a sense of purpose and meaning, as we work towards a common goal or mission.

Experience joy: Joyful community can provide opportunities for laughter, fun, and celebration, which can enhance our overall sense of joy and happiness.

Learn and grow: Being part of a community can expose us to new ideas, perspectives, and experiences, which can help us to learn and grow as individuals.

How to Build and Sustain a Joyful Community

Building and sustaining a joyful community requires effort and intention, but the rewards are significant. Here are some steps you can take to build and sustain a joyful community in your life:

Identify your values and mission: To build a joyful community, it's important to have a clear sense of your values and mission. What do you care about? What is the purpose of your community? Having a clear sense of purpose can help to attract like-minded individuals and create a sense of cohesion.

Build relationships: Relationships are the foundation of joyful community. Focus on building meaningful relationships with others, based on trust, respect, and authenticity.

Foster a sense of belonging: Create a sense of belonging by actively welcoming new members, acknowledging contributions, and providing opportunities for engagement and connection.

Celebrate and have fun: Joyful community should be fun! Create opportunities for celebration, play, and laughter.

Communicate effectively: Effective communication is essential for building and sustaining joyful community. Practice active listening, speak from the heart, and be open to feedback and ideas from others.

Collaborate and share resources: Joyful community thrives on collaboration and shared resources. Identify areas of common interest and work together to achieve shared goals.

## 33: JOYFUL COMMUNITY: BUILDING AND SUSTAINING A JOYFUL COMMUNITY

Be inclusive: Joyful community is inclusive and diverse. Strive to create a space where everyone feels welcome and valued, regardless of their background or identity.

Benefits of Joyful Community

Building and sustaining a joyful community in your life can lead to numerous benefits, including:

– Increased sense of belonging and connection

– Enhanced well-being and happiness

– Greater sense of purpose and meaning

– Opportunities for growth and learning

– More joy and laughter in everyday life

Conclusion

Joyful community is an essential aspect of our lives, providing us with a sense of connection, purpose, and joy. By identifying your values and mission, building relationships, fostering a sense of belonging, celebrating and having fun, communicating effectively, collaborating and sharing resources, and being inclusive, you can build and sustain a joyful community in your life. Remember, building a joyful community takes effort and intention, but the rewards are significant. Experience greater happiness and well-being by cultivating a joyful community in your life.

# 34: Joyful Reflection: Reflecting on Your Life for Greater Joy and Fulfillment

Joyful reflection is the process of taking time to reflect on your life, experiences, and emotions in a way that promotes greater self-awareness, clarity, and well-being. It allows you to gain insights about yourself, your values, and your goals, and to make intentional choices that align with your vision for a joyful and fulfilling life. In this chapter, we will explore the concept of joyful reflection, including its benefits, methods, and tips for integrating it into your daily routine.

Benefits of Joyful Reflection

Joyful reflection offers numerous benefits, including:

Greater self-awareness: Reflecting on your experiences and emotions can help you to gain a deeper understanding of yourself, your values, and your beliefs.

Clarity: By reflecting on your goals and aspirations, you can gain greater clarity about what you want to achieve and how to get there.

Enhanced problem-solving: Reflecting on challenges and setbacks can help you to develop effective problem-solving strategies and learn from your mistakes.

Increased gratitude: Joyful reflection can cultivate a sense of gratitude and appreciation for the good things in your life, which can enhance your overall sense of well-being and joy.

Improved mental health: Reflecting on your emotions and experiences can help to reduce stress, anxiety, and depression, and promote greater mental health and resilience.

Methods of Joyful Reflection

There are numerous methods of joyful reflection, and different methods may work better for different individuals. Some popular methods include:

Journaling: Writing down your thoughts, feelings, and experiences in a journal can be a powerful tool for reflection. It allows you to process your emotions, gain insights, and track your progress over time.

Meditation: Meditation can help you to quiet your mind, focus your attention, and gain clarity about your thoughts and emotions.

Mindful breathing: Taking a few moments to focus on your breath and connect with your body can help to calm your mind and promote greater self-awareness.

Gratitude practice: Taking time to reflect on the things you are grateful for can cultivate a sense of joy and appreciation in your life.

Reflection prompts: Using reflection prompts, such as questions or quotes, can help to guide your thinking and promote deeper insights.

Tips for Integrating Joyful Reflection into Your Daily Routine

To make joyful reflection a habit in your daily routine, consider the following tips:

Schedule time for reflection: Set aside a regular time and place for reflection, such as first thing in the morning or before bed.

Make it a ritual: Create a ritual around your reflection practice, such as lighting a candle or playing calming music, to make it feel more intentional and enjoyable.

Start small: Begin with just a few minutes of reflection each day, and gradually increase the time as you become more comfortable with the practice.

Experiment with different methods: Try out different reflection methods to see what works best for you, and don't be afraid to mix and match.

Be gentle with yourself: Remember that joyful reflection is a process, and it's okay to have ups and downs. Be gentle with yourself and practice self-compassion as you reflect on your experiences and emotions.

Conclusion

Joyful reflection is a powerful tool for promoting greater self-awareness, clarity, and well-being in your life. By taking time to reflect on your experiences, emotions, and goals, you can gain insights, make intentional choices, and cultivate a sense of joy and fulfillment in your daily life. Experiment with different reflection methods, be gentle with yourself, and make joyful reflection a habit in your daily routine. Experience greater joy and fulfillment by reflecting on your life with intention and purpose.

# 35: Joyful Legacy: Creating a Legacy of Joy and Meaning in Your Life

Introduction:

We all want to live a life that is filled with joy and meaning. We want to leave a legacy that will make a difference in the world and that will be remembered by future generations. But how do we create such a legacy? How do we ensure that our lives are not just a series of random events, but rather a deliberate and purposeful journey towards a joyful and meaningful existence? In this chapter, we will explore the concept of a joyful legacy and how you can create one for yourself.

Defining a Joyful Legacy:

A joyful legacy is the impact that you leave on the world that is filled with joy and positivity. It is a reflection of the life you lived, the choices you made, and the people you touched along the way. A joyful legacy is not about leaving behind material possessions or wealth, but rather about leaving behind a lasting impact on the world that will continue to inspire and bring joy to others long after you are gone.

Creating a Joyful Legacy:

Creating a joyful legacy is not something that happens overnight. It requires intentionality, purpose, and a commitment to living a life that is filled with joy and positivity. Here are some steps you can take to create a joyful legacy:

– Define Your Values:

Your values are the foundation of your legacy. They are the principles that guide your actions, decisions, and interactions with others. To create a joyful legacy, you need to first define what values are most important to you. This will help you make choices and decisions that are in alignment with your values and will ensure that your legacy reflects the person you truly are.

– Set Your Intentions:

Setting intentions is a powerful way to create the life you want to live. It involves visualizing the outcomes you want to achieve and setting goals that align with those outcomes. When it comes to creating a joyful legacy, you need to set intentions that align with your values and the impact you want to have on the world. This might involve setting goals around volunteer work, charitable giving, or other ways of giving back to your community.

– Live a Life of Purpose:

Living a life of purpose means being intentional about the impact you want to have on the world. It means aligning your actions and decisions with your values and intentions. To create a joyful legacy, you need to live a life of purpose that is focused on bringing joy and positivity to those around you.

– Cultivate Meaningful Relationships:

The people in our lives play an important role in shaping our legacy. To create a joyful legacy, you need to cultivate meaningful relationships with those around you. This might involve spending time with family and friends, volunteering in your community, or joining social clubs or organizations that align with your values.

– Give Back:

## 35: JOYFUL LEGACY: CREATING A LEGACY OF JOY AND MEANING IN YOUR LIFE

Giving back is an essential part of creating a joyful legacy. It involves using your time, resources, and talents to make a positive impact on the world. Whether it's volunteering at a local charity, donating to a cause you believe in, or mentoring someone in need, giving back is a powerful way to create a joyful legacy.

Conclusion:

Creating a joyful legacy is not something that happens by accident. It requires intentionality, purpose, and a commitment to living a life that is filled with joy and positivity. By defining your values, setting your intentions, living a life of purpose, cultivating meaningful relationships, and giving back, you can create a legacy that will make a positive impact on the world and inspire others to live a life that is filled with joy and meaning. Remember, your legacy is not just what you leave behind, it is the impact you have on the world while you are here. So, go out and create a joyful legacy that will make a difference in the world and bring joy to those around you!

# 36: Conclusion: Embracing Joy as a Way of Life

As we come to the end of this comprehensive self-help guide, it is important to reiterate the transformative power of joy in every aspect of our lives. Joy is not just a fleeting emotion that we experience occasionally, but a way of life that we can cultivate and nurture within ourselves.

Throughout this book, we have explored the different dimensions of joy and how we can incorporate them into our daily lives. We have learned that joy can be found in simple things such as nature, music, and laughter. We have also learned that joy is a choice that we make, and that we can choose to focus on the positive aspects of our lives rather than dwelling on the negative.

We have discussed the importance of self-care and setting boundaries to protect our joy and well-being. We have learned that acceptance of life's challenges is a necessary part of our journey towards lasting joy and fulfillment. We have explored the role of community in supporting and sustaining our joy, and we have seen how reflection can help us gain greater insight and appreciation for the joys in our lives.

# 36: CONCLUSION: EMBRACING JOY AS A WAY OF LIFE

Finally, we have discussed the importance of creating a legacy of joy and meaning in our lives. By living a life filled with joy, we can inspire others to do the same and leave a positive impact on the world.

It is our hope that this guide has provided you with the tools and inspiration to embrace joy as a way of life. Remember, joy is not a destination that we reach, but a journey that we embark upon each and every day. It requires intention, mindfulness, and a willingness to let go of the things that do not serve us.

As you move forward on your journey towards lasting joy and fulfillment, we encourage you to stay open to new experiences and opportunities for growth. Embrace the present moment, find joy in the small things, and always remember that you have the power to choose joy in every aspect of your life.

# Thank You

As we reach the end of this book, I want to say thanks for reading this book.

I want to get this information out to as many people as possible. If you found this book helpful, I would greatly appreciate you leaving me a review. This helps others find the book as well.

# Disclaimer

This document is geared towards providing exact and reliable information in regards to the topic and issue covered. The publication is sold on the idea that the publisher is not required to render an accounting, officially permitted, or otherwise, qualified services. If advice is necessary, legal, financial, medical or professional, a practiced individual in the profession should be ordered.

This information is not presented by a financial or medical practitioner and is for entertainment, educational and informational purposes only. The content is not intended as a substitute for professional medical advice, diagnosis, or treatment. Always seek the advice of your physician or other qualified health care provider with any questions you may have regarding a medical condition. Never disregard professional medical advice or delay in seeking it because of something you have read.

The information provided herein is stated to be truthful and consistent, in that any liability, in terms of inattention or otherwise, by any usage or abuse of any policies, processes, or directions contained within is the solitary and utter responsibility of the recipient reader. Under no circumstances

## DISCLAIMER

will any legal responsibility or blame be held against the publisher for any reparation, damages, or monetary loss due to the information herein, either directly or indirectly.

www.ingramcontent.com/pod-product-compliance
Lightning Source LLC
Chambersburg PA
CBHW060528130626
46553CB00002B/683